African Theatre
13

Series Editors
Martin Banham, James Gibbs,
Yvette Hutchison, Femi Osofisan
& Jane Plastow

Reviews Editor
Martin Banham
Workshop Theatre, School of English, University of Leeds LS2 9JT, UK

Associate Editors
Omofolabo Ajayi-Soyinka
Dept of Theatre, 1530 Naismith Dr, University of Kansas, Lawrence, KS 66045–3140, USA
Awo Mana Asiedu
School of Performing Arts, PO Box 201, University of Ghana, Legon, Ghana
David Kerr
Dept of Media Studies, Private Bag 00703, University of Botswana, Gaborone, Botswana
Amandina Lihamba
Dept of Fine & Performing Arts, PO Box 3505, University of Dar es Salaam, Tanzania
Patrick Mangeni
Head of Dept of Music, Dance & Drama, Makerere University, Kampala, Uganda
Christine Matzke
Dept of English, University of Bayreuth, 95440 Bayreuth, Germany
Olu Obafemi
Dept of English, University of Ilorin, Ilorin, Nigeria

Published titles in the series:
African Theatre in Development
African Theatre: Playwrights & Politics
African Theatre: Women
African Theatre: Southern Africa
African Theatre: Soyinka: Blackout, Blowout & Beyond
African Theatre: Youth
African Theatre 7: Companies
African Theatre 8: Diasporas
African Theatre 9: Histories 1850–1950
African Theatre 10: Media & Performance
African Theatre 11: Festivals
African Theatre 12: Shakespeare in & out of Africa
African Theatre 13: Ngũgĩ wa Thiong'o & Wole Soyinka

Forthcoming:
African Theatre 14: Contemporary Women

Articles not exceeding 5,000 words should be submitted preferably as an email attachment.

Style: Preferably use UK rather than US spellings. Italicize titles of books or plays. Use single inverted commas and double for quotes within quotes. Type notes at the end of the text on a separate sheet. Do not justify the right-hand margins.

References should follow the style of this volume (Surname date: page number) in text. All references should then be listed at the end of article in full:
Surname, name, date, *title of work* (place of publication: name of publisher)
Surname, name, date, 'title of article' in surname, initial (ed./eds) title of work (place of publication: publisher)
or Surname, name, date, 'title of article', *Journal*, vol., no: page numbers.

Reviewers should provide full bibliographic details, including extent, ISBN and price.

Copyright: Please ensure, where appropriate, that clearance has been obtained from copyright holders of material used. Illustrations may also be submitted if appropriate and if accompanied by full captions and with reproduction rights clearly indicated. It is the responsibility of the contributors to clear all permissions.

All submissions should be accompanied by a brief biographical profile. The editors cannot undertake to return material submitted and contributors are advised to keep a copy of all material sent in case of loss in transit.

Editorial address
African Theatre, c/o Jane Plastow, Workshop Theatre, School of English,
University of Leeds, Leeds LS2 9JT, UK • j.e.plastow@leeds.ac.uk

Books for Review & Review articles
Professor Martin Banham, Reviews Editor, *African Theatre*,
Workshop Theatre, School of English, University of Leeds LS2 9JT, UK
martinbanham@btinternet.com

African Theatre 13
Ngũgĩ wa Thiong'o & Wole Soyinka

Volume Editors
Martin Banham & Femi Osofisan

Guest Editor
Kimani Njogu

Reviews Editor
Martin Banham

JAMES CURREY

James Currey
is an imprint of Boydell and Brewer Ltd
PO Box 9, Woodbridge, Suffolk IP12 3DF (GB)

and of

Boydell & Brewer Inc.
668 Mt Hope Avenue, Rochester, NY 14620-2731 (US)
www.boydellandbrewer.com
www.jamescurrey.com

© Contributors 2014
© Playscript *A Rain of Stones* © Wole Soyinka

All Rights Reserved. Except as permitted under current legislation
no part of this work may be photocopied, stored in a retrieval system,
published, performed in public, adapted, broadcast,
transmitted, recorded or reproduced in any form or by any means,
without the prior permission of the copyright owner

The publisher has no responsibility for the continued existence or accuracy of URLs for external or third-party internet websites referred to in this book, and does not guarantee that any content on such websites is, or will remain, accurate or appropriate.

British Library Cataloguing in Publication Data
A catalogue record for this book is available on request from the British Library

ISBN 978-1-84701-098-8 (James Currey paper)

Typeset in 10/11 pt Minion Pro by Kate Kirkwood Cumbria, UK

Contents

Notes on Contributors   viii
Obituary of Pat Amadu Maddy   xi
Introduction by Martin Banham, Femi Osofisan & Kīmani Njogu   xiv

Reading & Performing African Drama   1
    How Wole Soyinka & Ngũgĩ wa Thiong'o influenced my work
    DAVID KERR

Ayan Contra *Ujamaa*   8
    Soyinka & Ngũgĩ as theatre theorists
    BIODUN JEYIFO

ENCOUNTERS WITH SOYINKA

I   Working with Wole Soyinka   17
    TUNJI OYELANA (in conversation with SOLA ADEYEMI)

II   The Difficulties of a Neophyte Staging   24
    Wole Soyinka's *The Beatification of Area Boy*
    TUNDE ONIKOYI

III   Pentecostalizing Soyinka's *The Trials of Brother Jero*   29
    BISI ADIGUN

IV   *The Lion & the Jewel* in Mombasa   32
    SILVIAH NAMUSSASI

ENCOUNTERS WITH NGUGI

I   Choru wa Mũirũrĩ   37
     Reflections on the Kamĩrĩĩthũ experience
     MUGO MUHIA

II   Producing *I Will Marry When I Want* in South Africa   42
     FREDERICK MBOGO

III   Ngũgĩ wa Thiong'o   48
     The unrecognized Black Hermit
     OBY OBYERODHYAMBO

IV   Kamĩrĩĩthũ in Retrospect   53
     GICHINGIRI NDIGIRIGI

Wole Soyinka & Ngũgĩ wa Thiong'o: Plays in Production   60
     JAMES GIBBS & MUGO MUHIA

The Making of *The Trial of Dedan Kĩmathi* by   77
Ngũgĩ wa Thiong'o & Mĩcere Gĩthae Mũgo
at the University of California, Irvine
     A personal reflection
     KETU H. KATRAK

Playscript   93
     A Rain of Stones
     WOLE SOYINKA

Book Reviews
Osita Okagbue on   110
New Plays from Africa
     Munyaradzi Mawere, *Rain Petitioning & Step Child*
     Kelvin Ngong Toh, *Fointama*
     Bole Butake, *Dance of the Vampires & Six other Plays*
     Francis Imbuga, *The Green Cross of Kafira*

Contents

Jane Plastow on
    Samuel Kasule, *Resistance & Politics in Contemporary*
    East African Theatre: Trends in Ugandan Theatre since 1960
	113

Christine Matzke on
    Astrid van Weyenberg, T*he Politics of Adaptation:*
    Contemporary African Drama & Greek Tragedy
	116

Jane Plastow on Galina Balashova, *Drama in Modern Ethiopian Literature & Theatre*	119

Colin Chambers on
    Bernth Lindfors, *Ira Aldridge: Vol. 3, Performing Shakespeare*
    in Europe, 1852-1855
	121

Laurenz Leky on
    Nadja Keller, Christoph Nix, Thomas Spieckermann (eds),
    Theater in Afrika: Zwischen Kunst und Entwicklungszusammen-
    arbeit: Geschichten einer deutsch-malawischen Kooperation /
    Theatre in Africa: Between Art & Development Cooperation:
    Stories of a German-Malawian Collaboration (Recherchen 106)
	122

Jane Taylor on Yvette Hutchison, *South African Performance & Archives of Memory*	125

Martin Banham on
    Kene Igweonu & Osita Okagbue (eds), *Performative Inter-Actions*
    in African Theatre
	127

Notice on a forthcoming title:

Femi Osofisan on
    Alain Ricard, *Wole Soyinka et Nestor Zinsou: De la scène*
    à l'espace public
	127

Notes on Contributors

Sola Adeyemi teaches drama, with special focus on African performance and contemporary British theatre, at the University of Greenwich, London.

Bisi Adigun received his PhD from Trinity College, Dublin in 2012. He is a playwright, theatre director and the founding/artistic director of Arambe Production (see www.aramebeproductions.com). Currently, he lectures at the School of Visual and Performing Arts at the Kwara State University, Malete – Ilorin.

Biodun Jeyifo is Emeritus Professor of English at Cornell University and Professor of African American Studies and of Comparative Literature at Harvard University. He was educated at the University of Ibadan (B.A.) and New York University (M.A., Ph.D.). He has taught at the University of Ibadan and the Obafemi Awolowo University, Ile-Ife (both in Nigeria) and at Oberlin College and Cornell University in the USA. He has lectured widely in Africa, Europe, North America and Asia. He has also served as an External Examiner in several African, European, Canadian, Caribbean and South Asian universities. Biodun Jeyifo has published many books, monographs and essays on Anglophone African and Caribbean writings, drama, Marxist and postcolonial literary and cultural studies. *Wole Soyinka: Politics, Poetics, and Postcolonialism* won one of the American Library Association's Outstanding Academic Texts (OATS) awards for 2005. The two-volume *Oxford Encyclopedia of African Thought* which Professor Jeyifo co-edited with Professor Abiola Irele was published in 2010. He is presently completing a monograph on 'Nollywood', the national video film industry of Nigeria.

Ketu H. Katrak, originally from Bombay, is Professor in the Department of Drama at the University of California, Irvine. Katrak has published widely in the fields of African Drama, Indian Dance, and Postcolonial Literature and Theory. She is the author of *Wole Soyinka and Modern Tragedy* (Greenwood, 1986), *Politics of the Female Body: Postcolonial Women Writers* (Rutgers UP,

Notes on Contributors ix

2006), and *Contemporary Indian Dance: New Creative Choreography in India and the Diaspora* (Palgrave Macmillan, 2011). Katrak is the recipient of a Bunting Fellowship (Radcliffe/Harvard), and a Fulbright Research Award.

David Kerr has lived most of his adult life in Southern Africa (working at universities in Malawi, Zambia and Botswana) where he practises theatre for human rights and social transformation. He has written widely on the topic (especially his book, *African Popular Theatre*) and has also published plays, a novel, stories and poetry.

Fredrick Mbogo teaches at Moi University's Department of Literature, Theatre and Film Studies from where he received a PhD after a dissertation on the interaction of aesthetics and pedagogy in popular drama on Kenyan television. Previously he received a Master of Arts degree in dramatic arts from the University of Witwatersrand. While at Wits he directed the play *I Will Marry When I Want*. He has directed other plays in both South Africa and Kenya in such venues at Wits Amphitheatre in Johannesburg, the Alliance Française and Kenya National Theatre in Nairobi as well as in other towns in Kenya.

Mũgo Mũhĩa teaches in Kenyatta University and specializes in Folklore, African Literature, Theory of Literature and Eco-criticism. He holds a PhD and B.Ed from Egerton University, Kenya, and an MA from the University of Nairobi.

Silviah Namussasi has been with The Theatre Company since 2011 and has been a facilitator at the *Story Moja Hay Festival Children's Theatre Workshop, Caroline Wambui Children's Home Theatre Workshop* and *Naro Moru Home* for the disabled, assisting colleagues in the project *Sanaa Ponyevu (Healing Art)*. She has performed in *Kimbia*, based on Kenyan Athletes, for which Silviah and her colleagues travelled to Eldoret for a hands- (and feet-) on experience and research to develop the play. She has also featured in *Shungwaya* and *Wanawake wa Heri wa Winsa* among other productions.

Gĩchingiri Ndĩgĩrĩgĩ is an Associate Professor of English and Africana Studies at the University of Tennessee, Knoxville. His most recent work on Ngũgĩ has appeared in *Approaches to Teaching the Works of Ngugi wa Thiong'o* and *The Canadian Review of Comparative Literature*. He was the Guest Editor for *Mũtiiri* (8). His edited collection of essays on the African dictator novel is forthcoming from the University of Tennessee Press.

Tunde Onikoyi teaches Film Production and Studies in Digital Culture in the School of Visual and Performing Arts, Kwara State University, Malete-Ilorin, Nigeria.

Tunji Oyelana is a multi-talented artist – a guitarist, actor, dancer, singer, composer, band leader, impresario – based in London. He is the founder and leader of the musical group *The Benders*, which has featured in many of Wole Soyinka's plays and films.

Oby Obyerodhyambo has taught literature at Kenyatta and Nairobi Universities. He is the author of several plays: *Positive Identity*, *Kit Mikayi*, *Drumbeats on Kerenyaga*, *Wanjiku's Dilemma*, *Striped Leopard*, and *La Femme Fatale* which have been performed in Kenya since 1986. He has acted and directed as a member of the Kenyatta University Creative and Performing Arts Centre and University of Nairobi's Free Travelling Theatre. Currently he works in the field of Public Health, using community theatre for mobilization and education.

Obituary
Yulisa Amadu Maddy

(27 December 1936–16 March 2014)

Yulisa Amadu Maddy, known as 'Pat Maddy', was a Sierra Leonean playwright, theatre company creator and director who had a major impact on theatre in Sierra Leone, and made contributions to theatre in the United Kingdom, Nigeria and Zambia.

Born in Freetown and educated at St Edward's Secondary School, Maddy travelled to Britain in 1958 where he trained at the Rose Bruford College of Speech and Drama. His play, *Yon Kon (Clever Thief)* was broadcast on the BBC's Third Programme and in the African Theatre slot on the African Service (21 February 1965). He worked as an actor in London, playing Chief-in-Town in the 1965 production of Soyinka's *The Road*. However, at some point after the 1965 production Maddy moved to Denmark, where he worked in radio and had a book of poetry translated and published: *Ny afrikansk prosa* (1969). The radio play mentioned above, together with *Obasai (Over Yonder)*, *Alla Gbah (The Big Man)* and *Gbana-Bendu (Tough Guy)*, were brought together in *Obasai and Other Plays* and published in Heinemann's African Writers Series (1968). Some of his work, such as *If Wishes Were Horses* (broadcast by the BBC (27 November 1963) remains unpublished, but *Life Everlasting* can be found in Cosmo Pieterse's collection of *Short African Plays* (1972).

Back in Sierra Leone at the end of the 'sixties, Maddy became Head of Radio Drama. Prompted by the vital role he ascribed to the arts, he founded 'Gbakanda Afrikan Tiata'. 'Gbakanda', meaning 'strength or endurance', was intended 'to bring all the arts together into a living reality for the people of Africa' and it came to life in the different countries in which Maddy worked. 1970 found him working in Zambia, where he prepared the Zambian National Dance Troupe for the Montreal World's Fair (1970) and for Expo '70 in Osaka. The challenge of working in Lusaka proved considerable and Michael Etherton, his patron who was already established in Lusaka, has referred to the difficulties Maddy had in 'coming to terms with the theatre' there (quoted in Currey, 2008: 83). After Expo '70, Maddy worked for a year in Osaka as a dance-theatre director, but by 1973 he was visible once again in London, where he directed *Gbana-Bendu* at the Keskidee Centre, Islington.

Maddy had submitted a novel, *No Past, No Present, No Future*, to Heinemann Educational Publishers and, according to James Currey, had 'responded to a series of tough reports on the text'. As a result, it joined his collection of plays in the African Writers Series (1973). During the mid-seventies, Maddy returned to Sierra Leone where he was both given weighty responsibilities and harassed because of his social concerns. According to David Kerr, the authorities objected to his 1976 play, *Big Berrin (Big Burying)*, which showed 'the brutality and degradation resorted to by the inhabitants of an urban slum' (Kerr, 1995: 251). During 1977, Maddy was Director of the Sierra Leone Dance Troupe and led the company to Lagos where it participated in the major cultural gathering of that year, Festac '77. On his return to Sierra Leone, he was imprisoned.

Eventually released, his health impaired as a result of torture, Maddy went into exile, moving initially to England where he re-established his theatre company. Gbakanda took *Pulse*, 'a psycho-political satire' by the Asmara-born Ethiopian Alem Mezgebe, to the Edinburgh Festival where it won a Fringe First Award.

The year 1980 found Maddy in Nigeria where he taught drama at the University of Ibadan and, once again, established Gbakanda Afrikan Tiata. A note in the programme for the group's first Nigerian outing reads in part: '... [Maddy's] approach [to re-establishing Gbakanda] was so unorthodox it quite frankly shocked many people, especially those in the Premier University (Ibadan). He did not limit his contacts to established drama groups or professional actors; he merely collected his actors as he found them.' The inevitably uneven group he gathered made its Ibadan debut with a double-bill consisting of *The Trials of Brother Jero* and *Pulse*. This was followed by *Big Breeze Blowin* (July 1980), a domestic drama by Maddy set among members of the African Diaspora living in South West London. The play involves both psychological and physical violence and ends with the stabbing of a policeman. During May 1981, and reflecting its broad cultural remit, Gbakanda promoted an exhibition of art work by Tunde Allen-Taylor in Ibadan.

During the last two decades, Maddy spent extended periods in the USA where he was at one point a Fulbright Scholar at the University of Maryland as well as spending a period of time at Morgan State University. Briefly, it can be said that he enjoyed an academic career in the course of which he published works with Donnarae MacCann on images of Africa, and on neo-imperialism in children's books

Maddy returned to Sierra Leone in 2007 to continue his research into the country's cultural heritage. He died in Choithram Memorial Hospital, Freetown, on 16 March 2014. The programme note by 'F.D.' from which I have already quoted provides a sentence that is worth reproducing here: 'Wherever he went Pat Maddy ... left two vivid and lasting impressions – that of a theatrical gadfly, a constant centre of controversy, questioning, probing, demanding, and that of a highly polished, versatile and successful performer and director.' He is remembered by many who were touched by his writing and by Gbakanda Afrikan Tiata.

(In preparing the above I have used the following sources: Maddy's novel, published with Heinemann (1973); James Currey's *Africa Writes Back* (2008); Simon Gikandi's *Encyclopedia of African Literature* (2003), and David Kerr's *African Popular Theatre* (1995). I have also drawn on the programmes prepared for Gbakanda Afrikan Tiata productions in London and Ibadan. It is to be hoped that more extensive research with access to records of Maddy's work in different countries will be encouraged and, in due course, published.)

James Gibbs

Introduction

MARTIN BANHAM, FEMI OSOFISAN & Guest Editor KIMANI NJOGU

The editorial team of *African Theatre* welcome Professor Kimani Njogu as a guest editor of this volume, which is devoted to the theatre of Wole Soyinka and Ngũgĩ wa Thiong'o. Kimani Njogu, formerly of Kenyatta University, is now an independent scholar, Director of Twaweza Communications in Nairobi, and publisher of *Jahazi*, a journal of the arts, culture and performance. He has brought us his wide range of contacts amongst the theatre community of Kenya, and his deep knowledge of the theatre of Ngũgĩ wa Thiong'o. Femi Osofisan, of the core editorial team, has brought together the material on the theatre of Wole Soyinka.

This volume opens with contributions from two of the most distinguished contemporary scholars of African theatre, David Kerr and Biodun Jeyifo. Kerr offers a personal response to the influence that both Soyinka and Ngũgĩ had on him as both scholar and practitioner. Biodun Jeyifo offers a preview of what is destined to be a major monograph, suggesting that although there are differences between Soyinka and Ngũgĩ as theatre theorists, there are strong resonances between them.

We then turn to individual encounters with the plays of Soyinka and Ngũgĩ. Tunji Oyelana, in discussion with Sola Adeyemi, talks of his long association with Soyinka, from the days of the Orisun Theatre in the 1960s, through the Nigerian civil war, and up to the present day. His own contribution to Soyinka's theatre through his work as a composer and musician has been of the greatest significance. What follows are three experiences of working with Soyinka's theatre: Tunde Onikoyi on the challenge of a 'neophyte' staging *The Beatification of Area Boy*, Bisi Adigun on his 'pentecostalization' of *The Trials of Brother Jero*, and Silviah Namussasi on adapting and staging *The Lion and the Jewel* in Mombasa. Turning to Ngũgĩ, it is not surprising that in the contributions of Mũgo Mũhĩa, Oby Obyerodhyambo and Gĩchingiri Ndĩgĩrĩgĩ the discussion focuses on Ngũgĩ and the Kamĩrĩĩthũ experience – an episode in the contemporary theatrical history of East African theatre that still resonates. Finally, Frederick Mbogo relishes the experience and describes the challenges of staging *I Will Marry When I Want* in South Africa.

Introduction xv

James Gibbs – whose documenting of Soyinka's work is legendary – joins with Mũgo Mũhĩa to offer a 'playography' of work by Soyinka and Ngũgĩ. Gibbs concentrates on the production history of Soyinka's great play *Death and the King's Horseman*. Mũgo Mũhĩa offers a detailed chronicle of productions of Ngũgĩ's plays internationally. This offers probably the most complete record of the staging of Ngũgĩ's plays, plus supporting critical material.

We then move to the most recent major staging of *The Trial of Dedan Kĩmathi*, by Ngũgĩ wa Thiong'o and Mĩcere Gĩthae Mũgo, at the University of California, Irvine, in March 2014. Ketu H. Katrak, offers a detailed and fascinating record of both the making of the production and the critical response to it.

Finally, as is our policy in AFRICAN THEATRE, we offer a complete playscript. We are grateful to Wole Soyinka for offering us *A Rain of Stones*, written for radio and first broadcast by the BBC in 2002. As a play made for radio, this is best 'read' with both the eyes and the ears! Soyinka uses sound in a dramatic, powerful and menacing way. The play's dedication is to the Algerian writer Tahar Djaout 'and all other victims of religious zealotry'.

Finally we offer a selection of book reviews.

The editors' thanks are expressed to our colleagues on the wider *African Theatre* editorial team, and to Lynn Taylor, our brilliant editor at Boydell & Brewer/James Currey.

MB. KN. FO.

Reading & Performing African Drama
How Wole Soyinka & Ngũgĩ wa Thiong'o influenced my work

DAVID KERR

This essay tries to pin down how a book or play influences a reader. Specifically I want to chart some of the influences that Wole Soyinka's *Kongi's Harvest* and *I will Marry When I Want* by Ngũgĩ wa Thiong'o and Ngũgĩ wa Mĩriĩ have had on me personally and on my theatre practice in Africa. I shall try to show how, in addition to a play's content, other determining factors are important, such as the age of the reader, the place where s/he reads the text, the performance or non-performance of the text and previous influences that the author has had on the reader. That is, a dramatist's influence is part of an extended conversation, debate or even argument with the reader/audience. I suggest also that, in an African context, influence is often a collective process which is not just a dialogue between author and reader, but an extended set of mutual influences between author and various interlocking audiences and readerships.

Wole Soyinka's *Kongi's Harvest*

The first time I read a sub-Saharan text of any genre was in 1963 as an undergraduate student in the library of Newcastle-Upon-Tyne where I stumbled upon the Oxford edition of *Five Plays* by Wole Soyinka. At the time I was dissatisfied with the traditional English 'lit. crit.' fare that I was being fed in the English Department lectures, and I proceeded to do a lot of extra-curricular reading of Asian, Caribbean and Latin American novels. Soyinka's *Five Plays* was the only sub-Saharan African text I could find. The first play I read in the collection was *The Lion and the Jewel*, which I enjoyed thoroughly, as I made mental comparisons with Molière and Goldsmith. My rather complacent pigeon-holing was completely shattered by the next play I selected, *The Strong Breed*, and even more confused by *The Swamp Dwellers*. I realized that if I were to make sense of these plays I would need far more extensive reading of African history, anthropology, sociology and literature. Over the next five or six years I made forays into this material, but it was in competition with other intellectual interests – Marxism, cultural studies, race relations, and environmental issues. My reading of black power texts (Angela Davis) led me onto Pan African texts – Du Bois, Padmore and Kwame Nkrumah, as well as Negritude poets, Césaire and Senghor. This pot-pourri of intellectual influences increased in intensity when I was accepted as a lecturer at the University of Malawi.

When I arrived in Malawi in 1969 the praxis of the Kamuzu Banda's one-party state and brutal techniques of detention without trial, as well as an omnivorous Censorship Board, shattered my eggshell-thin patchwork of intellectual radicalism. I rapidly found myself in a context where I had to make choices in the way I taught undergraduate students, who included such brilliant opponents of the regime as Jack Mapanje, Lupenga Mphande and Frank Chipasula. Ex-pat lecturers such a Landeg White, James Gibbs and myself had to find a path which would allow the student to express opposition to the regime without exposing them to detention, or what Mapanje called 'accidentalisation' (Mapanje 2004: 73).

I have discussed elsewhere the techniques of metaphor and allegory which the members of the Writers' Workshop and Travelling Theatre used to outwit the Censorship Board (Kerr 2012). Here I simply want to concentrate on the chosen texts of Soyinka and the two Ngũgĩs.

Soyinka's *Kongi's Harvest* was published by Oxford in 1967 (Soyinka 1967). It took three or four years before the text reached Malawi. As soon as I read it I realized the play would never get past the Malawi Censorship Board for performance, but it was also clear that it was a key text for Malawian intellectuals to read. The plot, dealing with a post-colonial dictator, Kongi, who uses a panoply of pseudo-traditional organizations and symbols to legitimize his brutal dictatorship, while a youthful opposition planned the dictator's downfall, perfectly fitted the Malawian regime. The following chart of motifs in the play and their parallels in Kamuzu's regime illustrates the relevance of the allegory in a Malawian context.

Kongi's Harvest	Kamuzu's Dictatorship
Kongi Highway	Kamuzu Highway
Kongi Stadium	Kamuzu Stadium
Carpenter's Brigade	Young Pioneers
Eyes & Ears of the State	Special Branch (later Special Intelligence Services)
Segi's father	Masauko Chipembere – major opponent of Kamuzu
Segi (former lover of Kongi, now Daodu's Lover)	The People (once supporting Kongi, now supporting younger generation of rebels)

Although Chancellor College Travelling Theatre (henceforth CCTT) could not mount a production of such a play, it was possible to have it on the literature syllabus, where the parallels between the play and the realities of Malawi hardly needed pointing out. The more I taught the text, the more I realized its complex theatricality. One of the weaknesses of much African literature of the 1960s and early '70s was its reliance on 'the man of two worlds' motif – the young man (rarely woman) whose education allows him to straddle the world of Africa and the Euro-American north. This simple binary between tradition and modernity neglected ways in which rural traditions have adapted to and sometimes resisted modernity.

The attraction of *Kongi's Harvest*, especially with my orientation towards a Marxist analysis of culture, was its dialectical structure. Instead of a simple tradition/modernity contrast, *Kongi's Harvest* posits a dialectical interpretation of tradition and modernity. In the first section, 'Hemlock', we see that Danlola's polygamy and love of traditional music fit into a typical 'Af. Lit.' view of tradition, but Danlola's delaying tactics in refusing to offer the New Yam to Kongi show that Danlola is not only able to resist Kongi, but to understand the complexities of modern politics. The dialectic which Soyinka uses to structure *Kongi's Harvest* is not a simplistic thesis, antithesis, synthesis; it is complicated by the untidy reality of West African culture. Soyinka provides a symbolical framework which illustrates his thematic preoccupations.

Danlola/Old Awerri	Kongi/New Awerri	Segi's Father/Segi/Daodu
Old Yam, plentiful food, agricultural fertilty	New Yam, poor harvests, fasting, hunger	New Yam, plentiful food, agricultural fertility using modern farming methods
Sexuality, fertility, polygamy	Abstinence, destruction, sterility	Sexuality, fertility, procreation, monogamy
Rich cultural heritage, traditional music and dance (sincere praise songs)	Mediated culture (radio, photos, simplistic music, forced praise songs)	Nightclub music and dance of lovers
Life, tolerance, continuity	Death, militaristic culture, dictatorship, torture	Life, tolerance, selective change, multi-culturalism

The intertwined themes of fertility, sexuality and resistance to neocolonialism articulated well with my interests in Marxism, South African politics, ecology and gender issues.

I Will Marry When I Want by Ngũgĩ wa Thiong'o and Ngũgĩ wa Mĩriĩ

The influence of *I Will Marry When I Want* (henceforth *Marry*) came from a later period in my life, the late 1970s and 1980s. From 1974 to 1980 I was artistic Director of Chikwakwa Theatre at the University of Zambia. I tried to build on the theatre methodology initiated by such activists as Michael Etherton and Mapopa Mtonga. This entailed using the Unzadrams Travelling Theatre to 'take theatre to the people' by visiting different provinces each year with a selection of plays in both English and the local Zambian language. Etherton had been deported in 1972, though not for his theatre activities; nevertheless there was some sensitivity about drama, especially with Zambia being an important Front Line State in the struggle against colonialism in Angola, Mozambique, Zimbabwe and Namibia, and against Apartheid in South Africa.

With the help of Mtonga and Zimbabwean exile, Stephen Chifunyise, we expanded the Travelling Theatre work to include workshops to build the skills in schools and teacher training colleges. We also made contact with some of the Laedza Batanani workers in Botswana such as Ross Kidd, Jeppe Kelepile and Martha Maplanka; these activists were implementing what came to be called Theatre for Development Methodologies, influenced by the theories and work of Paolo Freire and Augusto Boal. In 1977 two Laedza Batanani workers joined our Travelling Theatre trip to Luapula province.

1977 was the year that Ngũgĩ wa Thiong'o was detained for a year because of his involvement in the theatre of the Kamĩrĩĩthũ Educational Community Centre (henceforth KECC). I had of course been immersed in Ngũgĩ wa Thiongo's earlier writing, particularly his novels, *A Grain of Wheat* and *Petals of Blood*. I was also intrigued by the way the play he wrote with Mĩcere Mũgo, *The Trial of Dedan Kĩmathi*, included Brechtian techniques, which were more sophisticated than Ngũgĩ's earlier realistic style.

There is no need to elaborate the tumultuous events of the following four years in Kenya: Ngũgĩ wa Thiong'o's release, his return to Kamĩrĩĩthũ, the withdrawal of the permit to perform, the creation of a new play, and eventually in 1981 the destruction of the theatre by government forces. This was followed by death-threats to some of the main facilitators, and their eventual dispersal: Ngũgĩ wa Thiong'o to USA, Ngũgĩ wa Mĩriĩ, Mĩcere Mũgo and Kimani Gecau to Zimbabwe. Gecau and wa Mĩriĩ settled in Zimbabwe and worked closely with Zimbabwean theatre worker Stephen Chifunyise (recently arrived from exile in Zambia); they became the driving forces behind the formation of Zimbabwean Association of Community Theatres, ZACT.

In 1982, the English versions of *Marry* and *Devil on the Cross* (the novel that Ngũgĩ wa Thiong'o secretly wrote in prison) were both published, and I managed to get copies of the texts shortly afterwards. At about the same time, he wrote several articles about the 'epistemological break' with bourgeois thinking that his prison experiences had helped to engender. He later collected these papers in *Decolonising the Mind* (Ngũgĩ 1986); this too became essential reading among Malawian intellectuals.

Some books (such as *Kongi's Harvest*) had an instantaneous impact on me; others have had a long-term effect, like waves hitting the sand. *Marry* falls in the latter category. At first, I had reservations about the play for its blatant use of a melodramatic plot, with Kĩoi playing the role of the villain; Kĩgũũnda, the victim who suffers from the manipulative techniques of Kĩoi; and Gĩcaamba, the hero who stands up for the rights of the peasants (and acts as the mouthpiece for the authors). I recognized, however, that the actual performance must have hit chords within the hearts of the mostly peasant audience, backed up as it was by Brechtian stagecraft and the use of songs to signpost the connection between the 1950s and the 1980s. Flashbacks to the Kenyans' struggle against colonialism are ironically juxtaposed with the comprador capitalists' oppression of peasants in the post-colonial period. The Ngũgĩs also effectively relate both colonial and neo-colonial forms of domination to the role of Christianity, which they saw as a conduit for bourgeois hegemony.

One of the biggest innovations of Ngũgĩ wa Thiong'o and Ngũgĩ wa Mirii was an insistence on creating plays in Gĩkũyũ and other Kenyan languages, and ensuring that plays be published in Gĩkũyũ before being translated and published in English. For theatre workers in Zambia, this was not a major step, since the UNZADRAMS Travelling Theatre had already been using local languages in their devised plays in rural areas since 1969. In the urban areas, however, English or multi-lingual plays were the norm, owing to potential audience tensions if one Zambian language was privileged over another.

When I returned to Malawi in 1981 (under the mistaken belief that Malawi was becoming more tolerant of opposition), my colleague Chris Kamlongera took up my suggestion that we use chiTumbuka and chiChewa for a workshop in Mbalachanda, Mzimba District, funded by GTZ, a German NGO (Kamlongera 1984). This worked very well and the next step was to use chiChewa in some of our 'domestic' performances in Zomba and the surrounding areas. At first there was resistance on campus, as audiences had become used to plays in English, but soon the popularity of plays in chiChewa spread like wildfire throughout the country, with scores of community theatre groups emerging. I believe one of the motivating forces for this was the availability of *Marry* in Malawi, and I put the text on the reading list of a new course called 'Theatre for Development'.

The growing student interest in a class analysis based on the Kamĩrĩĩthũ experience had its impact on other types of theatre in which the CCTT was involved. The Theatre of Development projects that we set up with the help of GTZ started off as purely technocratic, instrumental theatre advocating the use of hygienic wells and toilets. However, it gradually developed into a much more radical critique of a rural class system, which was the ultimate cause of existing deficiencies in sanitation (Kerr 2002). This never reached the confrontational level that the Kamĩrĩĩthũ Cultural Centre achieved in Kenya, but the latter provided what was almost a bench-mark for theatre companies trying to make their performances relevant to the injustices in society.

The inspiration of *Marry* on Malawian student theatre workers continued throughout the 1980s in a cat-and-mouse game between the Travelling Theatre militants and the combined forces of the police and Censorship Board. In 1984 two of these radical students were detained without trial, but released after a year of campaigning by Amnesty International and other human rights organizations. This did not deter the students. Over the following years, two major plays, *Mmemo* (in chiChewa) and *They Call it Africa* (in English and chiChewa) had their permits removed, the former for its representation of labour laws and issues, the second for a scene revealing the almost slave conditions of contract workers on Malawi's tobacco estates. Other plays had scenes cut out after the Censorship Board became aware of the impact they had on audiences.

One other way in which *Marry* influenced class struggle in Southern Africa was through international networking. I mentioned the numerous theatre workshops which took place in the spread of Theatre for Development. Many of these were funded by NGOs, and a debate began to emerge about the extent to which Theatre for Development should advocate the insurrectionary motives advocated by the Ngũgĩs. Unsurprisingly, most NGOs took a negative view of such activities.

There were moves, however, to provide an international channel for theatre which advocated working class and peasant causes. At an international conference in Bangladesh in 1983, an attempt was made to set up a global network of radical theatre workers: the International Popular Theatre Alliance (IPTA). Ngũgĩ wa Mĩriĩ (recently exiled from Kenya), Mtonga, and myself among others represented African theatre. Asian representatives dominated the meetings, but there were important inputs from Caribbean, Latin American and Canadian delegates. A modest journal was established under the temporary editorship of a Zambian, Dickson Mwansa. Ross Kidd, Canadian veteran of Laedza Batanani, was given the job of establishing a database before handing over in a rotational system to Karl Gaspar from the Philippines.

The initiative was very short-lived. Just as Gaspar was due to start his office, he was arrested and detained without trial under the regime of Marcos (Gaspar 1992). Many delegates from other Asian countries received various forms of harassment. I suffered what I called 'postal arrest'; all my international mail stopped arriving. After the fall of the Banda regime I discovered from the Postmaster General that my correspondence was systematically confiscated by security agents who checked all mail before it was distributed. One of the personal, positive consequences for me was that I developed a good friendship with Ngũgĩ wa Mĩriĩ, which we were unable to foster through mail but through various academic or private visits I made to Zimbabwe.

By the beginning of the 1990s the conflict between many sectors of Malawian society (including most religious bodies) and the Malawian Government was reaching a climax. Western donors (after the release of Nelson Mandela and the unbanning of South African liberation movements) dissociated themselves from their former ally (Kamuzu Banda) and responded to human rights organizations. As a result, the Malawi government was pressured into releasing many political detainees, including the well-known poet, Jack Mapanje (Mapanje 2011).

It is perhaps fitting that the last production of the Travelling Theatre before the university was closed down in 1992 was a dramatized version of the novel that Ngũgĩ wa Thiong'o had written in prison: *Devil on the Cross*. The play was ready for performance just at the moment when there was a student demonstration against the government. The police came onto campus and the university was closed; a permit was refused for future performances. In a sense it didn't matter. The drama of protests and street demonstrators was more influential than anything that could be performed on a stage.

My conclusion about the impact the works of Soyinka and Ngũgĩ have had on me is that the influence is far from being a simple communication in private between author and reader. It is filtered through performances, the shared reaction of colleagues and students, and most of all, the praxis of theatrical activism. It is always difficult to assess the impact a book or play has on events, but I'd like to believe that the two plays I have highlighted, by spreading the tentacles of their beliefs and artistry far into the continent, did contribute to positive changes in Africa, an influence that still continues even as circumstances change.

REFERENCES

Gaspar, Karl (1985). *How Long?: Prison Reflections of Karl Gaspar*, Quezon City: Claretian Publications.
Kamlongera, Chris (1984). *Theatre for Development in Africa with Case Studies from Malawi and Zambia*, Bonn: Deutsche Stiftung fur Internationale Entwicklung.
Kerr, D. (2002). 'Theatre and Social Issues in Malawi: Performers, Audiences, Aesthetics', in Harding, F. (ed.) *The Performance Arts in Africa: A Reader*, London and New York: Routledge, 311-20 [reprint].
────── (2012). 'Playing the Tyrant Away: Creative Academic Resistance to Dictatorship in Malawi', *Journal of Arts and Communities*, 2/3: 215-25.
Mapanje, J. (2011). *And Crocodiles are Hungry at Night: a Memoir*, Banbury: Ayebia Clarke Publishing.
Ngũgĩ wa Thiong'o (1986). *Decolonising The Mind: The Politics and Language of African Literature*, London: James Currey, Portsmouth, NH: Heinemann, and Nairobi: Heinemann Kenya.
Ngũgĩ wa Thiong'o and Ngũgĩ wa Mĩriĩ, 1982, *I Will Marry When I Want*, London: Heinemann Educational Books.
Soyinka, Wole (1967). *Kongi's Harvest*, Oxford & New York: Oxford University Press.

Ayan Contra *Ujamaa*
Soyinka & Ngũgĩ as theatre theorists

Prolegomenon to a monograph on the cultural archives of revolutionary theories of theatre & modernity in Africa

BIODUN JEYIFO

Ayanlaja and *Ayangbemi*:
the poetics of a *longue durée* of expertise and mastery

Ayan is the Yoruba god of music and patron deity of the arts of drumming. His name stands as a prefix in the patronymics of families and lineages either devoted in earlier times to his worship or descended from great practitioners of the art and practice of drum music: Ayanniyi, Ayandele, Ayanlaja, Ayanwole, Ayanbiyi. Like many other African peoples, music was and remains a central aspect of the ritual, festive and daily lives of Yorubas. For this reason, Ayan, the god of music, is one of the most ubiquitous deities in the Yoruba pantheon, even though he is not as widely acknowledged and celebrated as those other great male and female deities of the Orisa tradition like Ogun, Sango, Ifa, Orunmila, Osun, Oya and Yemoja. Two of the Ayan-derived patronymics that I find particularly illustrative of the values and significations associated with this god are *Ayanlaja* (Ayan resolves conflicts; he brings peace to warring individuals and groups) and *Ayangbemi* (I have found favour in the god; in Ayan, my blessings are manifold). In these names are great conceits, perhaps even fabulous catechisms: music, under the patronage of Ayan, can bring peace to a troubled world and can serve as the ultimate beatitude for an individual or a people.

To the extent that music is an essential part of the worship of all the deities, Ayan as patron god of music is indispensable to the worship of all the deities. Once, in a rare find in the archives of the Music Library of Cornell University, I discovered recordings by William Bascom from the early 1950s of the musical repertoire associated with each of the principal Yoruba deities, complete with glosses written by the great cultural anthropologist himself. In each case, the musical performance was done by some of the most celebrated *Bata* and *Dundun* musical groups of the period.

At the climax of ritual worship when a god manifests himself or herself through a possessed devotee, Ayan is the agent, the medium of the epiphany.

This is achieved not haphazardly but with great attention to pacing, timbre, tonality and nuance in the orchestration of the music, for the drummers, singers and chanters are highly trained and very skilful performers. With master drummers in particular, they not only come from lineages redolent with long-departed and celebrated master drummers of the past, they themselves begin their training from very early in life and ply their trade and craft for their entire lives. And with long training and cultivated skills come professional pride and a cultural authority that make the great master drummers some of the most venerable men in their towns or villages. Many of these master drummers may be part-time farmers and hunters, but first and foremost, they are musicians, they are the elect of Ayan, the divine patron of all musicians. Above all else, the master drummers, their assistants and apprentices belong to craft guilds parallel to the guilds of hunter-warriors, priests and diviners and blacksmiths. Just as the guild of hunter-warriors has responsibility for maintenance of peace and security and the organization of the hunt, so the guild of drummers and musicians, under the patronage of Ayan, has responsibility for performing music for all occasions, from the most specialized and cultic to the most secular and mundane.

As students of his works know only too well, in Wole Soyinka's theoretical writings on drama and theatre the myths and rituals of the gods are superabundantly present, but not Ayan, who is notable for his complete absence in Soyinka's appropriations of the gods and their cultic rituals for a radical theory of modern African drama and theatre. Ogun, the god of iron, war and revolution, is nearly omnipresent in this genre of the non-fictional prose writings of the Nigerian playwright. Next to Ogun's ubiquity are the considerable musings of Soyinka on Obatala, Sango and Oya, especially in his long essay 'Drama and the African Worldview', one of the four that comprise the collection, *Myth, Literature and the African World*. Incidentally, Esu gets a mere nod of acknowledgment in these theoretical writings of Soyinka, a grudging acknowledgment that is exactly counter to Esu's centrality in the theoretical and dramatic writings of Femi Osofisan and Femi Euba. All three, Soyinka, Osofisan and Euba, make no mention at all of Ayan.

I suggest that the reason for this silence, this either wilful or accidental forgetting of Ayan and the centrality of his assigned patronage of music and musicians, is quite uncomplicated: that which is so obvious, so all-pervasive, tends to be taken for granted. In the following long passage from 'The Fourth Stage' (1994b), perhaps Soyinka's most important theoretical essay on drama and theatre and definitely his most widely read, the paean to language and music, to music as primal vessel to language, is nothing other than a tacit celebration of Ayan, even though the ritual alluded to in the passage is thematically related to Ogun's primal dare of the nothingness that preceded and forever haunts Being:

> Language in Yoruba tragic music therefore undergoes transformation through myth into a secret (masonic) correspondence with the symbolism of tragedy, a symbolic medium of spiritual emotions with the heart of choric union. It transcends particularization (of meaning) to tap the tragic source whence spring the familiar

weird, disruptive melodies. The masonic union of sign and melody, the true tragic music, unearths cosmic uncertainties which pervade human existence, reveals the magnitude and power of creation, but above all creates a harrowing sense of omnidirectional vastness where the creative Intelligence resides and prompts the soul to futile exploration. The senses do not at such moments interpret myth in their particular concretions; we are left only with the emotional and spiritual values, the essential experience of cosmic reality. (Soyinka, 1994b: 31)

Many scholars and critics of Soyinka's writings have commented, often negatively, on the unyielding difficulty or even obscurity of the language, the *English*, of many of his creative works in general and of his theoretical writings in particular. I imagine that to such scholars and critics, this passage is vintage Soyinka. But as I have argued elsewhere, the alleged difficulty or obscurity of Soyinka's theoretical and critical writings, whatever the merits of the charge with regard to any particular piece of our author's writings, reflects some scholars' preference for clear, lucid styles of writings in general and of African writings in particular (Jeyifo, 2004). Thus, with regard to this quoted passage from 'The Fourth Stage' a sympathetic reading would quite easily reveal that in the very texture of the passage, Soyinka is *enacting* what he is arguing, this being the idea that at certain levels of performative sublimity, music is far more powerful than language in opening up for us intimations that referential words cannot evoke, cannot reveal. The *themes* of the ritual drama that climaxes with these intimations may belong to the primal agency of Ogun but the *achievement* of the ineffable through tragic music is the work of Ayan and his acolytes.

In his greatest plays, as in his theoretical writings on drama and theatre, Soyinka presupposes a centrality, in realizing the right aesthetic sensibilities and achieving the appropriate texture of performance, of collaboration with drummers and musicians under the patronage and guidance of Ayan, with the best training and technical skills available in the culture. *A Dance of the Forests, The Road, Kongi's Harvest, Madmen and Specialists* and, above all other plays, *Death and the King's Horseman*: every single one of these plays is inconceivable as a performative piece without highly skilled drummers and musicians whose enabling imprimatur is etched in such varied incarnations of the god of music as *Ayansola* (Ayan dispenses joy, festivity, celebration); *Ayanjare* (Ayan secures and consolidates justice and rectitude) and *Ayandoye* (Ayan transmits knowledge and wisdom).

With regard to philosophical themes, at the heart of Soyinka's theoretical writings on drama and theatre is the idea that life and existence are ineradicably riven by conflicts and contradictions that must be addressed, must be transcended. Indeed, the notion of a 'fourth stage' in the major essay of the same title is precisely an inscription of this idea derived from myth and ritual, that within the chasms between time past, time present and time future and within the unbridgeable divides between past, present and future generations, that 'fourth stage' is a bridgehead that enables heroic protagonist actors to dare to annul or transcend these rifts. But with the possible exception of *A Dance of the Forests*, the gods and their rituals that so pervade the theoretical writings of Soyinka are as a matter of fact generally absent in the action and *dramatis personae* of his plays. In other words, his dramatic works are not suffused by gods, deities and avatars. Only the musical and performative idioms associated with the gods' cults and rituals survive into the plays. Thus, Ayan may never have received even a single mention in his theoretical writings, but in the incorporation of beautiful or even sublime cultic music and ritual into the dialogue dramas of the Nigerian playwright, Ayan, I suggest, is the presiding spirit.

Ujamaa: a demotic poetics of unity and collectivism

I think it is safe to say that next to the word *Uhuru* which means freedom, the most widely known and used word in the Swahili language is *Ujamaa*. Thanks to the writings of Julius Nyerere like *Ujamaa – Essays on Socialism* and *Uhuru Na Ujamaa – Freedom and Socialism*, together with his policies while he was President of Tanzania as well as the popularization given the word by its incorporation into the guiding principles of Kwanzaa, the most important African-based cultural holiday and festival among African Americans, *Ujamaa* has become a household word throughout the African world. With etymological roots in the Swahili term for family togetherness and community unity, *Ujamaa* has come to mean the achievement of personhood and identity primarily through one's connection to the collective good of the community. This does not mean the effacement of selfhood or the repression of individuality; rather, it means that personhood and collectivity are dialectically related; one achieves its fullness and agency through the other in mutually reinforcing and sustaining relations.

Without ever directly invoking the word itself, modern discourses on the heritage of culture and the arts in Africa are saturated by values and ideas associated with *Ujamaa*. In poetry, music, dance, sculpture, oral narratives and verbal rhetoric, the idea of creations for and by the community acting in unity for the common good holds a commanding, even venerable position among scholars and practitioners devoted to a common racial-continental heritage in African arts. The accent is on anonymous creators working not to elevate themselves and their talents above everyone else but to fulfill themselves as creative people by the quality of approval they elicit from their communities. Skill, talent and idiosyncrasies are acknowledged and even celebrated, but only insofar as they are not touted as accomplishments that elevate individual artists and performers above everyone else. More crucial is the idea that skill and talent are widely distributed in the community and are, at any rate, easily reproducible. From this arises the view that the arts have value only to the extent that they enhance collective survival and uphold communal solidarity.

As with Soyinka's complete silence on Ayan even as the god and his significations implicitly pervade his theoretical writings on theatre and drama, it is in vain that one looks for an invocation of the word *Ujamaa* in the powerful essays of Ngũgĩ wa Thiong'o on his work in the theatre separate from but not discontinuous with his primary interest in the novel. I place emphasis here on the centrality of his work in the famous Kamĩrĩĩthũ Community Education and Cultural Centre in Kenya as both the object and the bench mark of Ngũgĩ's theoretical reflections on theatre. This is because his own work in the Kamĩrĩĩthũ Centre is about the only theatrical expression on which Ngũgĩ has based all his reflections on the theatre. He mentions other playwrights like Francis Imbuga, Kenneth Watene and Mĩcere Mũgo of Kenya and directors and theorists of modern European theatre like Peter Brook and Jerzy Grotowski. But it is almost exclusively on the work he did at Kamĩrĩĩthũ with peasants and workers on which Ngũgĩ theorizes. And from beginning to the end, he goes to an extraordinary length in downplaying his own talent and his own vision while simultaneously highlighting the contributions of the ordinary men and women of the village of Kamĩrĩĩthũ in the creation of modern Africa's most famous progressive community theatre. In this regard, the following passage from the essay, 'The Language of African Theatre', one of the chapters in the controversial book of essays, *Decolonising the Mind: The Politics of Language in African Literature*, is fairly characteristic of the demotic nature of the theorizing that we encounter in Ngũgĩ's reflections on the theatre:

> Auditions and rehearsals for instance were in the open. I must say that this was initially forced on us by the empty space but it was also part of the growing conviction that a democratic solution even in the solution of artistic problems, however slow and chaotic it at times seemed, was producing results of a high artistic order and was forging a community spirit in a community of artistic workers. PhDs from the University of Nairobi, PhDs from the university of the factory and the plantation, and PhDs from Gorki's 'university of the streets' – each person's worth was judged by the scale of each person's contribution to the group effort. The open auditions and the rehearsals with everybody seeing all the elements that went into making a whole had the effect of demystifying the theatrical process. (Ngũgĩ, 1986: 56)

The notion of demystifying the theatrical process with which Ngũgĩ concludes his observations in the passage goes to the heart of the author's theory of revolutionary community theatre. This is because virtually everything in the work of the Kamĩrĩĩthũ Centre in making theatre the centre of its educational and civic programmes was created collectively, from the plays that were performed to the casting of roles for the characters to the determination of formal questions of relations between form and content and relations between performers and their audiences. Workers and farmers who had never done any work in the 'legitimate' theatre, who had little or no formal education, and who actually learnt things in the very process of creating them dominate the claims made by Ngũgĩ for a practice of a revolutionary community theatre project that started from scratch, from completely new beginnings. Well, not exactly, for many of the songs, dances and stories that went into the making of the two plays produced, *Ngaahika Ndeenda* (*I Will Marry When I Want*) and *Maitũ Njugĩra* (*Mother, Sing for Me*), came from the community members themselves. In this way, *Ujamaa*, as the spirit of the Ngũgĩs' theatre work in the Kamĩrĩĩthũ

Community Education and Cultural Centre, was as much an inspiring idea as it was the achieved result of the efforts of the theatre workers.

Ayan and *Ujamaa*: the discontinuities and continuities of the bourgeois revolution and the peasant-worker revolution in modern African theatre

We can easily perceive that Soyinka and Ngũgĩ occupy two extremes in theoretical discourses on modern African theatre. Let us slightly shift the terms of our reflections in these notes from 'modern African theatre' to 'theatre and modernity in Africa'. This is because for both men, theatre has long existed in Africa; it did not come to the continent and its peoples on the heels or in the wake of modernity. That is not the bone of contention, so to speak. The radical differences pertain to theatre and modernity in Africa. On this point, Soyinka is not as explicit as is Ngũgĩ on where his ideological and theoretical priorities lie. This is because Ngũgĩ is everywhere insistent that as far as theatre is concerned, modernity in Africa lives or dies with workers and farmers especially, but more generally with the dispossessed of all strata of the lower social orders leading the way. For him, the unity and communalism of *Ujamaa* are solidly class-based. By contrast, Soyinka's faith, as quiet as it is kept, is in a radical-liberal bourgeoisie of gifted and conscientious individuals and groups. Before starting his career as a playwright and theatre director, he had made a comprehensive study of the heritage of theatre and the arts in Africa and had discovered highly evolved and differentiated traditions of performance. As a counterpart or continuation of this, his first theatre groups, the '1960 Masks' and 'The Orisun Theatre', were made up of mostly middle-class professionals and petty-bourgeois university students.

The extreme radical difference in class and ideology between the two is best expressed in the question of language and African drama, or more precisely, language *in* African drama. Soyinka is openly dismissive of Ngũgĩ's insistence that language in African drama can and must be only the languages that workers and farmers and the masses of ordinary Africans use. The Nigerian playwright's stage English is a powerful refutation of Ngũgĩ's conflation of linguistic empiricism with realism as a mode of expression in dramatic dialogue. Soyinka's most memorable plays have characters who use or, rather *spout* a stage English which is a highly stylized mélange of how people generally really speak English in Nigeria and how the most erratic and idiosyncratic individuals use English within the context of the country's constitutive and ineradicable multilingualism. Of especial note is the fact that Soyinka's most stunningly poetic use of stage English bears unmistakable marks of idiomatic, lyrical Yoruba. This, I contend, is an expression, in the modern African context, of a bourgeois revolution in the means of linguistic and artistic production. All the same, Ngũgĩ's absolute insistence that a community theatre that is based almost solely on workers and farmers and the lumpen proletariat for both performers and audiences must use their languages is incontrovertible.

Against the compelling background of these differences between Soyinka and Ngũgĩ as theatre theorists, it may come as a surprise to find that there are resonances between them. Soyinka's theatre work has not faced the full force of state violence and repression that Ngũgĩ's work at Kamĩrĩĩthũ faced. But in the 'Before the Blackout' series and The Guerilla Theatre Unit of the University of Ife Theatre that Soyinka formed in the 60s and 80s respectively, workers, rural dwellers and the masses of ordinary people in some Nigerian cities, towns and villages found their grievances, interests and outlooks powerfully represented. In the Ngũgĩ that we encounter in the long essay, 'Enactments of Power: The Politics of Performance Space', perhaps his most engrossing theoretical discourse on theatre, is remarkably close to the Soyinka that we encounter in *his* essay, 'Theatre in Traditional African Cultures: Survival Patterns' (1994a). In both essays, there are moving accounts of the repression and interdictions that theatre and theatre people have faced in both colonial and postcolonial Africa, just as there is in both essays a confident affirmation of the often ingenious tactics and strategies that theatre artists and groups devise to keep working. Without any amnesia regarding assertions generally deemed authoritative that both the bourgeois revolutions and the worker-peasant revolutions belong to the past, I would argue that in the theoretical writings of Soyinka and Ngũgĩ we discover that in Africa as in many other parts of the developing world, they are not only alive, they are simultaneously discontinuous and continuous.

Biodun Jeyifo
Ibadan, Nigeria and Cambridge, Massachusetts

BIBLIOGRAPHY

Jeyifo, Biodun, (2004). *Wole Soyinka: Politics, Poetics and Postcolonialism*, Cambridge University Press.

Ngũgĩ wa Thiong'o (1986). 'The Language of African Drama', in *Decolonizing the Mind: the Politics of Language in African Literature*, London: James Currey.

—— (1998). 'Enactments of Power: The Politics of Performance Space', in *Penpoints, Gunpoints, and Dreams: Towards a Critical Theory of the Arts and the State in Africa*, Oxford: Clarendon Press.

—— (1986) and Ngũgĩ wa Mĩriĩ, *I Will Marry When I Want*, London: Heinemann, 1986.

Nyerere, Julius (1971). *Ujamaa – Essays on Socialism*, Oxford: Oxford University Press.

—— (1976). 'Drama and the African Worldview' in *Myth, Literature and the AfricanWorld*, Cambridge: Cambridge University Press.

—— (1990). *Uhuru Na Ujamaa – Freedom and Socialism*, Oxford: Oxford University Press.

Soyinka, Wole (1994a). 'Theatre in Traditional African Societies: Survival Patterns', in *Art, Dialogue and Outrage*, New York: Pantheon.

—— (1994b) 'The Fourth Stage', in *Art, Dialogue and Outrage*, New York: Pantheon.

Encounters with Soyinka

I
Working with Wole Soyinka

TUNJI OYELANA, in conversation with
SOLA ADEYEMI

Tunji Oyelana spoke to Sola Adeyemi at Emukay Restaurant, Camberwell, London, in April 2014. Oyelana is a long-time collaborator and was a member of Wole Soyinka's groups in the 1960s. In this interview, he reminisces about the early days of *Orisun Theatre* and his roles in the company up to the start of the Nigerian civil war in 1967.

First encounter with Wole Soyinka

My story with 'Prof.' (Wole Soyinka) started in 1960. I was the Private Secretary to Chief Kosoko of Lagos and was also managing his elementary school, Oba Kosoko School, which was situated on the ground floor of [the] palace. I was the headmaster and a teacher, and I was also taking care of the Chief's correspondence and organizing his administration. I spent about seven months working for Chief Kosoko, and suddenly, one day, the phone rang and the voice at the other end said he was Wole Soyinka. Now, I had heard about the man; the topic of my comprehension examination in the Cambridge School Certificate was Wole Soyinka. That was how I got to know about anybody called Wole Soyinka at that time; I had never heard of him before my examinations. But I had known his entire family, although I didn't connect him with the family. Even when I started working with him, I didn't relate him with the Soyinka family that I knew in Abeokuta. The father, Essay, (Samuel Ayodele Soyinka) was the Headmaster of St Peter's School, Ake, Abeokuta. His mother (Mrs Grace Eniola Soyinka) was a very generous woman and had a lot of attributes that Soyinka inherited – Mama's sense of humour was huge! She was very cheerful, very easy to talk to, and many people don't know that Soyinka is also very approachable. So, I knew the father, I knew the mother, I knew the senior sister – Sister Tinu – who was at the Abeokuta Grammar School when I was at St John's elementary school, Igbein, Abeokuta, because our house was right opposite the grammar school and she used to come to our house every school [day], and even on some Saturdays. Next door to our house was another bungalow where one woman sold food and the grammar school students used to eat in the tent in front of the woman's house. The ladies, whom I shall refer to as being from the elite class in Abeokuta, were provided with a bench and a long table in our compound, about six of them. Sister Tinu would send me to collect her food from the woman, Mama Ijebu, to eat in our compound, not in the woman's tent. So, I got to know her and later knew what family she came from in Ake. Then I knew Buoda Femi (Wole Soyinka's immediate junior brother); he was my senior and a school prefect when I was in Class 2 at Abeokuta Grammar School. He told me Sister Tinu was his sister. So, I could connect those two Soyinkas. The one after Buoda Femi, Yeside, was my classmate; we entered the grammar school in 1954. The last one that I knew then was Kayode Soyinka. So, I knew all the members of the family apart from Folabo, who was much younger.

When I read about this playwright, I did not link it to the family, because there was another Soyinka family in Abeokuta. In the same year at Abeokuta Grammar School, apart from Yeside Soyinka, there was also Biodun Soyinka who is a professor of Agriculture now, but they were not related.

Secretary to *1960 Masks*

When this man spoke to me on the phone and said he wanted to interview me, my reaction was, 'for what?' He told me to come and see him. How he got to know about me, we have never spoken about till today. I have cracked some jokes in his presence to see whether he would respond but he has never reacted. Anyway, I went for the interview in the flat of Miss Laide Idowu (later Mrs Soyinka) at Surulere, Lagos. Miss Idowu was then teaching at a girls' grammar school in Yaba and maintained the flat; Soyinka used to stay in the flat any time he was in Lagos.

At the interview, Soyinka spoke to me about a drama group called the *1960 Masks* and said he wanted to find a secretary for the group. He asked me what I did as Secretary for Chief Kosoko. I told him. Soyinka told me straightaway that he found me appropriate to be appointed as Secretary to '60 *Masks*. I was very glad and even more so when I asked about the salary. He told me; it was clearly almost double what I was earning at Chief Kosoko's, and more than double what civil servants of my calibre were earning. I was already earning about £5 more than clerks in the civil service. Yet, I found it difficult to leave Chief Kosoko. The man loved me like one of his children. He was very sad when he heard that I was leaving but he was stoical about it and released me.

In any case, Soyinka did not give me time to think about the offer. He wanted me to start the following day. At that time, he was based at Ibadan as the Rockefeller Research Fellow and he told me I would be moving to Ibadan as that is where the company would be based, though my relocation was not going to be immediate. At that time, '60 *Masks* was rehearsing a new production – *You in Your Small Corner* – *A Dance of the Forests* had just finished. There was a link between '60 Masks and AMSAC (American Society of African Culture) which was founded as a result of the congress of Negro Writers and Artists in 1956. The Society sponsored a two-day festival in Lagos in 1962, so '60 Masks was using AMSAC premises for rehearsals. Members of '60 Masks from Ibadan were coming to Lagos every alternate weekend, and those in Lagos were going to Ibadan on the other weekends to rehearse at Obisesan Hall in Ibadan. That was before we started using the premises of Mbari at Ogunpa Oyo, near Westend Café, a Lebanese restaurant. Westend Cafe owned the premises; the owner of the house, Mr Hadad, was using the upper floor of the restaurant and we had the bungalow at the back and the courtyard for rehearsals and productions. Soyinka later turned the place into a kind of amphitheatre.

First productions

My first assignment with the group was the rehearsal of the Jamaican dramatist Barry Reckord's *You in Your Small Corner*, a play that tried to represent the Caribbean migrant experience in London. We did this before doing *Song of a Goat* and *Trials of Brother Jero* at the courtyard of Lagos Museum at Onikan. This was after Soyinka decided that we should bring in younger artists to form *Orisun Theatre*. I was coordinating everything as the Secretary of *1960 Masks*, and I was travelling everywhere with him in his Land Rover because he was also writing and I was his secretary as well as being the secretary of '60 Masks. He would be driving and dictating to me.

Soyinka's writing style

This was a completely new experience to my life. Soyinka was busy all the time. He had things that had to be written down all the time. The process honed my ambition to learn, to know English better as a subject; it fuelled my wish to be able to speak and use English like him. There is a little anecdote here. When he was writing *The Interpreters*, I had to type the first line of the novel more than eight times. Each time, Soyinka would correct – 'Metal on concrete jars my drink lobes' – and each time I would try to rewrite it, thinking that the man had made an error. Yet, he was tolerant; he didn't complain but would cross out my additions and emendations and return the page to be retyped. He did not bother to verbally correct me until I correctly typed it as he wanted. That was one of my earliest experiences with him and his way of working. I learnt the painstaking nature of his writing. Some of the poems and plays that I had typed in the early 1960s were not published until much later. Years later. He would go over the scripts several times with different coloured pens, and sometimes, a few years later, he would suddenly call you to do further work on an old script. Take *The Interpreters* for instance. I typed the script in 1960 to 1961. You can imagine my surprise when he gave me the manuscript again in, I think, 1964 to correct. Yes, painstaking patience. Even *Kongi's Harvest* was not published until just before the war, I think, in 1967 (or maybe the war had started by then, I cannot be sure). Those works must have gone through seasoned revisions because, for him, there is no shoddy work. Everything has to be perfect, and that is what he expects of you in everything. Although some of the later works such as *King Baabu* and *The Beatification of the Area Boy* at Africa 95 seemed not to have gone through that kind of process because before they were staged, there had been several readings and workshops. As you know, *Area Boy* was like a revue, with several sketches that deal with different issues. Although he found a common thread to structure everything together.

Rehearsal techniques

That was also his style of directing. He won't correct you but would expect you to bring out your own interpretation of the play, to use your imagination. That was when I realized that the man did not want me as secretary at all. He wanted me to use my talent and skills, to develop my talents. Being a secretary was to make me earn money but the main reason for getting me into *1960 Masks* was to make me use my talents where I was everything in the group – apprentice set constructor, musician, stage manager, administrator, coordinator, etc.

Soyinka was also compassionate. When I moved from Lagos to Ibadan, he lodged me at Chief Segun Olusola's house in Bodija and that became one of our bases in Ibadan. Bodija was sparsely populated then and we had several places then that we used as offices for *'60 Masks*. I was working out of a briefcase most of the time.

I had a cousin in Ibadan who was also a member of *'60 Masks*; Segun Sofowote was a Presenter at WNBS/WNTV (Western Nigeria Broadcasting Service / Western Nigeria Television). He had a house in Ibadan and that is where I lodged. Segun and I were involved in all aspects of *'60 Masks* because, by the time I joined the group, about eight members of it, including Tayo Ayorinde (now the Oba of Sabo) and Femi Euba had already left for England. Soon, Segun also left, leaving only me in the *'60 Masks*. That's how I came to be the very first member of the Orisun Theatre and the one who invited others for auditions, from Wale Ogunyemi, Jimi Johnson, Jimi Solanke to Yomi Obileye. They later became indispensable members of *Orisun Theatre*. Those who had no jobs were given something to do at Mbari, and every single member was encouraged to become more educated in the theatre.

Orisun Theatre

The *Orisun Theatre* was born because the *'60 Masks* members were leaving the country and the group was becoming defunct. Segun Olusola became too busy; he joined another group called *Players of the Dawn* with Christopher Kolade.

Yemi Lijadu had already left NBC (Nigerian Broadcasting Corporation) for UNESCO in Paris and Ralph Opara had been transferred to Eastern Nigeria as the Controller of the Eastern Nigeria Broadcasting Service. And some of the women became more occupied with their government work. When Soyinka realized that the group was going to disintegrate completely, he decided to form another group to affiliate with what was left of the company. But the members of the '60 Masks were still coming to act with members of the Orisun Theatre, doing collaborative productions, till they all left.

The audition for the new group was advertised widely in Ibadan and more than eighty people turned up. It was held at the big compound of Quarter 86 in Agodi, where Soyinka was living then. Out of the attendees, he was able to bring in between 14 and 16 people for the training programme. Prof invited teachers from the University of Ibadan to teach us: Ebun Odutola (now Professor Ebun Clark) and Funmilayo Sowunmi (later Ajose-Ajayi) were taking us [in] Speech (Elocution and Phonetics) because Speech was very important to Soyinka. Dapo Adelugba taught stagecraft. Joel Adedeji came later. Akin Euba was also coming to interact with us for Music. Soyinka himself took us [in] Mime, Acting and Movement. The training was strenuous, lasting sometimes up to 15 hours in the day. And it became even more strenuous during the rehearsal for *The Lion and the Jewel*.

Kongi's Harvest was also tough. Gaius Anoka was Kongi; Paul Worika had the stature but Soyinka preferred Anoha. He knew what he wanted from the play and designed and directed [the] production, as he did to the premieres of all his plays at this time. Dexter Lyndersay realized the set and designed the lighting. Soyinka had his own concept for sets, costume and music. He wrote all his own music and gave me the scripts to interpret. I'll tell you a story. During the rehearsal of *Kongi's Harvest*, Soyinka gave Segi's song to several of us to interpret. We were in the Arts Theatre that day and each artist was going up to sing his own version, accompanied by the drums or guitar. When it came to my turn, I sang only two lines and the noise in the house couldn't let me continue! And Soyinka said, 'Stop, stop, stop. That's it! Print.' *Omi tó tòrò ninini, la fi bó'jú è!* [1] That was how I became *Orisun's* de facto musician.

Of course, I did a lot of compositions for Soyinka's other plays too over the years but he was always very knowledgeable about the music and other concepts for his work. Let me tell you another story: at the time he was teaching us music and dance at Agodi Quarters, we were trying to deceive him, thinking the man would not know the cultural dances and songs. He would watch you for a while before asking you to do it again, properly this time. At that time, I thought I could even deceive the man with music but it was a lie! He knew all that was necessary; he played the double bass guitar, he played drums, he knew his notes, but he acknowledges your talents and he wanted fresh ideas to add to his own concepts. Kongi does his own compositions but at times, he needs fresh ideas. *O fe ki talent e yen wa added to his own efforts*. [2] That's one thing I have noticed about him; he wanted to expose your talent in the theatre too.

Although, later, when Soyinka was at Ife (University of Ife, now Obafemi

Awolowo University), I couldn't leave Ibadan. But Jimi Solanke was at Ife and he was doing the music for the productions, with Wole Alade. But Jimi was the major person that he relied upon at Ife. However, when he wanted to record the album of *Unlimited Liability Company*,[3] he invited Tunji Oyelana and the Benders to do the music. I am happy that I was able to work with him for so long, and I gained a lot of things from working with him. As I said, I gained patience also.

Orisun Theatre did a lot of productions, including plays that had been done previously by '60 Masks – *The Lion and the Jewel*, for instance, and *The Strong Breed*. *Orisun* started from *Trials of Brother Jero* and *Song of a Goat* before doing *Kongi's Harvest*. Members of '60 Masks, such as Ralph Opara, Aig Imoukhuede and Yemi Lijadu, were in *Trials of Brother Jero* and *Song of a Goat*, and *The Republican* satirical sketches, which took place at Glover Hall, Lagos, [and] Lagos Museum and Arts Theatre, Ibadan. One of the reasons for forming *Orisun* was to create a kind of repertory theatre for Ibadan, to be based at the university. Soyinka found that he couldn't use students for the sustenance of that kind of theatre; he had to be able to have his own troupe that could move at any time and be dedicated to rehearsals and performances. If he was not detained during the war, we would not have seen the gradual disintegration of that group. Funding dried up during this time although Dapo Adelugba tried his best to keep the group together. We did a lot of weekly programmes on the television to earn some money and keep the group together.

The Road (1965)

I was the Director of Music for *The Road* at the Royal Stratford Theatre production in London. That was in 1965. I was also the lead singer in the band, among the motor park touts. We came from Ibadan then to augment the actors from London. I brought two people with me for the orchestra – Jimi Johnson and Bayo Oduneye. Jimi was on the drums while I played the guitar and sang the songs. Bayo played maracas. Femi Fatoba had been in London before then but I co-opted him into orchestra. There were other actors such as Rudolph Walker. During the performances, Prof informed me that some people were interested in the brand of music that I played and would like to do some recording sessions with the band. Of course, we had been doing that kind of performances for the WBNC/WNTV in Ibadan and getting paid £3 per 30-minute slots, so it was not a new thing. My only fear then was that we would be too tired, playing for long before the night's performance. But I was surprised that the sessions lasted only five minutes. Five minutes, and we were paid £26, each! This was with the BBC (British Broadcasting Corporation). Soyinka did poetry reading with Chris Okigbo, J. P. Clark and Cosmo Pieterse who had just arrived from South Africa then; he was South African. I coordinated back-up music for each session, and that is where I met some other South Africans, who helped in the production of my first singles in London. They played backing instruments for the singles; talents like Mokwoena, and Chris McGregor, who played saxophone. We recorded six sessions, in which we accompanied the poetry performances. Prof acknowledged the importance of the music to the readings, and how music is a very important adjunct to his writing. And generally, that was how my music became somehow linked to his writing since then. Even now, I feel humbled that Prof still calls on me to do the music for his plays. And when he calls, I don't refuse him. Next week, I'll be going to Lagos to perform at the Lagos Black Heritage Festival that he is directing. Yes, our relationship, or my association with Soyinka practically directed the course of my own professional path, since 1960.

Coda

If I have any regrets at all, it would be that we didn't record most of what we did then for posterity. And then the war came and Prof was detained. When he came out, when he was released, he needed some time to recuperate, to regain his old self... you should have seen him when he came out of prison – he had lost about a third of his weight. It was sad. Anyway, when he came out, he left the country to rest. He of course disbanded *Orisun Theatre* before he left the country.

NOTES

1 'Clear as a crystal is the water used to wash her face.' This was the chorus to the song in the night club scene of *Kongi's Harvest*. See Wole Soyinka (1967), *Kongi's Harvest*, Oxford University Press, 13-18.
2 'He wanted to acknowledge your contributions.'
3 *Unlimited Liability Company*. Featuring Tunji Oyelana and His Benders, Music and Lyrics by Wole Soyinka. Ewuro Productions, EWP 001.

II
The Difficulties of a Neophyte Staging
Wole Soyinka's *The Beatification of Area Boy*

TUNDE ONIKOYI

It was in the year 2003, towards the end of October that as an undergraduate student at the University of Ibadan, I decided to produce and direct Wole Soyinka's *The Beatification of Area Boy*. I was not a directing student, but every undergraduate in the department of theatre arts at that time had the liberty to venture into any area of the creative arts that caught his or her interest. To a very large extent, I believed that I was ripe for such a task because I have always been a firm believer in learning both the theory and practice of the theatrical and dramatic arts. This issue of marrying theory and practice was very significant because it was my understanding of the two, as inspired by that veteran scholar, Professor Dapo Adelugba, that challenged me to want to stage Soyinka's *Beatification of Area Boy*.

Casting

One of the many challenges I had for the casting was in the use of greenhorns and a crop of newly admitted students into the department. When I found myself in this precarious situation I knew and recall telling myself that I was in for my most difficult task ever. For I did not want to stage Soyinka just for the fun of it; rather, I wanted to prove to other students, especially those that specialized in directing, that you could tackle any of Soyinka's plays without fright.

Up till that time not one of my colleagues dared put up any major Soyinka play. They would give the usual clichés as an excuse. You would hear all sorts of discouraging remarks powerful enough to put you off the domain of Soyinka's plays. The best you would have observed from the boldest of these directing students would perhaps be plays like *Lion and the Jewel*, *Child Internationale* or *Trials of Brother Jero*; that is, the simpler plays that pose no serious challenge. Even of these plays, I saw only a few productions in the three years I spent as an undergraduate.

For my production, I had to make use of fresh students who had never encountered Wole Soyinka's work in all their life, except perhaps at secondary school level, where at best, they had read his poem, *Telephone Conversation*. Some of these students who found his style and language too complex backed out disappointingly. Those who agreed to stay asked me to cast them in the least demanding roles. With all this initially discouraging attitude from students whom I felt came to the university to work hard for a degree, I had to act fast and re-strategize to salvage the situation before things got out of hand.

First and foremost therefore, I went to seek the assistance of competent acting students who could take the roles of the principal characters such as Sanda, Miseyi, M.C., Barber, Judge, Military Boy, and Boyko. Thus Adebayo Shobakin played my Sanda, while Niyi Stephen MacMusa, a reliable actor, doubled in the same role. Three of my colleagues at the 400 level, namely Yomi Oguntoyinbo, Manfred Eche and Tunji Adewunmi were also very committed and helpful in the roles of Bridegroom, Military Boy and M.C. respectively. Fortunately for me too, although Judge and Miseyi were played by greenhorns, it was not difficult getting them into the world of the Soyinka work, as they themselves were keen to learn and go through the rigours of the profession. Most of the less committed newcomers, however, developed cold feet about the project, and only reluctantly played the roles of the downtrodden of the Maroko slums.

Rehearsals

I have personally learnt that one of the most important ways of staging plays written by Wole Soyinka is by adopting a systematic style of rehearsals. This rehearsal must come in several stages. This was also not a simple task, because as I said above I had to deal with a whole lot of inexperienced actors. Rehearsing a group of thirty-five students for such a play was a Herculean a task. I adopted the Adelugba style of holding consistent readings for a long time so that my actors could familiarize themselves with the story and get a full grasp of what the Nobel Laureate had in mind.

(i) Reading Beatification of Area Boy *as a work of literature*
We embarked on a preliminary discussion of the play as literature. This was necessary because we were dealing with a play that I felt needed to be understood first as literature, and then later as theatre. In treating the work as literature, I introduced the cast to the theme, subject matter and structure of the play, alongside the playwright's other works, especially his political plays. We went through character analyses, and discussed the locations that were either realistic or imaginary, relating these places as much as possible to the immediate reality of the Nigerian people. With this first reading, which took a month, half of my problems were virtually solved. The students were able to have a deeper understanding of the work as literature and also, in practical terms, to appreciate it better as a work of theatre.

(ii) Reading The Beatification of Area Boy *as a work of the theatre*

There is a saying that for a play to be well understood it has to be staged. While this aphorism is true to some extent, a theatre director knows that the play's closeted state has its own potential which must be appreciated before he or she decides to stage the work. *The Beatification of Area Boy* is a masterpiece that captures a brutal moment in our not too distant past in Nigeria – the era of the most vicious military dictator, General Sani Abacha. As a Nigerian director, no one needed to tell me about the kind of man he was, or of the various atrocities he committed. Many of my cast members were equally familiar with the events recorded in the play, and so found it not too difficult to re-enact them on stage.

Treating the work as literature first meant helping the students to have a feel of their individual roles before having to interpret them on stage. Being inexperienced actors for the most part, they were inclined to render their lines as if reciting the national anthem or pledge. So I had to make them understand that they were to be no longer themselves but other characters entirely, the playwright's created characters. I told them to imagine themselves not acting at all but actually living as the play's characters, and to try as much as they could to internalize the roles. I refused to give movements or blocking at the beginning. Learning to render the lines appropriately before blocking is for me a very significant step, for it allows the actor to come to a greater understanding of his or her role in relation to the other actors in the play generally. The process went on till the end of the second month and, through this less stressful approach to rehearsals, my actors became even more committed than they were before.

(iii) *Learning the songs and integrating them into the play*

Another challenge for us was in rendering Soyinka's music. The songs were meaningful and reflected the essence of the play, but they were entirely new to the cast. Giving tunes to the lyrics therefore became a major challenge for the newcomers. With the exception of some familiar songs that could pass as classical Yoruba allegro, most of the others were in English. These we had to recreate by giving them new tunes without subverting their intended meaning. The student actors eventually found this exercise enriching and enchanting, no doubt because songs have a way of speaking deeply to the soul.

I then decided to constitute the entire cast, both the speaking and non-speaking actors, into an ensemble, with everyone participating in all the areas of acting, dancing and singing. Our production of *The Beatification of Area Boy* thus turned out to be a good example of total theatre on the modern stage.

Set, costumes and props

This is an area I found extremely challenging. While the play gives opportunities for the use, for the most part, of an empty space or just some makeshift set, the sliding door to the supermarket remains the most problematic to achieve since it is not easy to build a sliding door on stage. At best what one could do in this regard was to get a wooden panel that could glide on appropriate castors, and that was what we did.

As for costuming, we were fortunate to be working in a place close to the play's location. Otherwise it would have cost us a lot to invest in all the costumes for the production. But as it was, we were able to rent or borrow what we needed. The same applied to stage properties, decor, make-up kits, and so on. The problem is that people are not used to investing in such significant things in this part of Africa.

The production

The production ran for four nights, each of them with its own experiences, and lessons. The first night was long and boring. The audience, which had anticipated a spectacular production with real professionalism, went away disappointed. The second night was better, and earned us some praise though not without its own amount of negative criticism. The third night was another disaster following the sudden absence of the actor playing the major character, Sanda. I had to turn in desperation to his double, Mr MacMusa, who was still struggling with his lines. MacMusa went on stage with his script but even with that nothing good came out of it. That third night has been my worst experience as a student director. It taught me that it is very significant to have double casting for certain roles. While as a director you hope for the best, it is always better to play safe and not leave anything to chance on the matter, because some unexpected event such as mine may ruin your plan for a successful production. The fourth and last night however went beautifully. The absent actor came back, and the play ran without a hitch, making it our best night.

Conclusion

In conclusion, I believe that it always advisable, in order to make the production of a Soyinka work succeed, to have a long-term plan. Unfortunately, directors run away from Soyinka's work because they do not have the patience and perseverance for such long-time planning. But if they are ready to adopt this approach, they will be happy with themselves afterwards. I for one consider myself fortunate to have had the opportunity of knowing Soyinka and his works well enough, from his most sublime and esoteric, to his most existentialist works.

Today, I teach film and no longer stage plays and, as a film teacher, have to devote my time to writing scripts for the screen. In line with this, I look forward indeed to the day when I will be able to adapt any of Wole Soyinka's works for the screen. Of all the playwrights in Nigeria, it is his works that have so far enjoyed the highest number of screen adaptations. *Kongi's Harvest*, for instance, was shot in 1970 by Francis Oladele, directed by Osie Davies; and in 1984, *Blues for a Prodigal* was filmed by Ugboma, Balogun and Soyinka himself with amateur actors. At the time of writing this peace, Soyinka's childhood memoir, *Aké: the Years of Childhood* is being shot at various locations by Dapo Adeniyi and Yemi Akintokun. All this notwithstanding, my greatest joy will be to see Soyinka's plays on stage and in front of a live audience.

III
Pentecostalizing Soyinka's *The Trials of Brother Jero*

BISI ADIGUN

In February 2009, I decided to produce Soyinka's comedy, *The Trials of Brother Jero*. It was to celebrate the fifth anniversary of my company, Arambe Productions, (Arambe), Ireland's first African theatre company. Mindful of my Irish audience, particularly the feminists, who could (mis)construe Soyinka's comedy as a creative endorsement of domestic violence or wife-battering, I decided to adapt it, using what I termed 'the pervasive phenomenon of Pentecostalism' in modern-day Nigeria as a backdrop. I sought and obtained Soyinka's permission, and immediately went to work.

Instead of a Brother Jero, a charlatan Bar Beach prophet, the protagonist in my version is Pastor Jero, a psychology graduate and a founding member of the Fountain of Flame Pentecostal Church. My Chume is well spoken and Amope, his wife, is also a university graduate. However, I heightened her aggressiveness to the point where she becomes a caricature, duly deserving of the spiritually sanctioned spanking for which Chume is seeking the permission of Pastor Jero to eventuate. The performance of the new version, which ran for nine days at the Samuel Beckett Theatre, inside Trinity College Dublin, was warmly received by critics and audiences alike. While Irish people represented the largest number in the audience, many Nigerians and other African people could also be seen nightly in the auditorium.

In April 2009, I was invited to Nigeria to direct my Pentecostal Jero for the benefit of Nigerian audiences using Nigeria-based actors. The production was a tripartite collaboration between Arambe, the University of Lagos, and the National Theatre. Little did I know when I was booking my flight to Nigeria that the performance of the play was the National Theatre's offering for the 2009 Democracy Day, which happened to fall on the 30 May 2009. I would like to briefly share my experience of returning home, after having lived in Europe as at 2009 for a total of 16 years, to produce, in collaboration with UNILAG and the National Theatre, what I had publicized in Ireland as a modernization of Soyinka's *The Trials of Brother Jero*.

The audition and rehearsal for the performance took place at UNILAG, Akoka. It had also been agreed that the play would preview for two nights at the

Main Auditorium at UNILAG before it transferred to the National at Iganmu for a four-weekend run, culminating in the final performance on Democracy Day. While we were rehearsing at UNILAG, I dealt directly with Professor Duro Oni, who was then the Head of Department of UNILAG's Creative Arts. Rehearsals went smoothly with little or no intervention from Oni.

But when it was time to make the poster to publicize the performance, Oni suggested to me that I should perhaps consider changing the title of my version somewhat for the Nigerian production. I insisted that for consistency, as well as posterity, I would rather the Nigerian production was advertised as it was advertised in Ireland: '...Presents Wole Soyinka's *The Trials of Brother Jero*. Modernised and Directed by Bisi Adigun'. As is the custom with Oni, he did not make any fuss about my insistence on being consistent.

Surprisingly, when the National Theatre presented a draft design of the poster to me for my perusal, it read: '...Adapted and Directed by Bisi Adigun'. I felt this was not right because, as I had made clear to Oni, the new version had already been premiered in Ireland and it was advertised as 'Modernised by'. So, I asked Professor Ahmed Yerima, who was then the Director of the National Theatre and the National Troupe, why the change from 'Modernised by' to 'Adapted by'? His response was that Soyinka would be upset if he saw the advertisement carrying 'Modernised by'. Bearing in mind the Yoruba proverb: 'One cannot shave a person's head in his/her absence', I decided to contact Kongi himself.

I met Soyinka one-on-one for the first time in 2006 in Palo Alto in California at the launch of his memoir, *You Must Set Forth at Dawn*. Not only did I have a handshake with the Nobel Laureate, I also had the opportunity to spend some minutes with our WS back-stage before I ushered him on stage with a Yoruba song, to the accompaniment of my djembe drum. Thereafter, I asked for his email address; and I had since kept in touch with him. Hence, the reason I did not hesitate to send an email to Soyinka to ask him if he would be upset if the proposed National Theatre's production of my version of his play were to be advertised as 'Modernised by...' In less than twenty four hours, I received Soyinka's response:

> I do not understand this word 'upset'. 'Offended', I do understand, or 'repelled'; etc. etc. Theatre is not a stomach as in 'stomach upset'. There are theatre conventions. 'Adapted by' is one, and it covers 'modernised by', 'deconstructed by', 'genderised by' etc. etc. So why the fuss?

It was the humour contained in this email that ultimately diffused the tension that was brewing over how my version should be advertised. Isn't it true that what a child could not see standing up is clearly visible to an elder sitting down? I stopped fussing over the word used to advertise the play and started focusing on how to make the performance a memorable one for actors, audience and my two collaborators. Needless to say that it was advertised by the National Theatre as 'Adapted by' and it was well received by all, regardless.

It was a few years later that I would come across Yerima's insightful book, *Basic Techniques in Playwriting*, in which he eloquently describes adaptation as:

'when playwrights make suitable plays already written, for new surrounding or audience, for a greater appeal'. Had Yerima said this to me, instead of insinuating that Soyinka would be upset if my version was advertised as a 'Modernised by', would I have made any fuss over my version being advertised as an adaptation? Not at all!!

The long and short of this story, however, is that after all the fuss I had made about not wanting to change the title of my version of Soyinka's comedy, I have since officially renamed it, *Haba Pastor Jero*!!!! to distinguish the adaptation from the original. So much for my insistence on consistency for the sake of posterity.

IV
The Lion & the Jewel in Mombasa

SILVIAH NAMUSSASI

In December 2013, I took responsibility for a Kenyan production of *The Lion and the Jewel* at the Little Theatre in Mombasa. This show was the first step and project that I took into the world of directing and I must say it was quite an experience. After I finished my Trainer of Trainees level of performance training, The Theatre Company of Kenya (TTC) put me in charge of the project as the director. I have always had an interest in directing but didn't know it was going to come that soon. With TTC overseeing the whole process, I worked closely with Cyrus Ng'ang'a, who was the dance choreographer, and Hillary Namanje, who was the company's Coastal Manager.

The show required a lot of energy and physical fitness and thus required a flexible team of ten actors with the crew included. Every rehearsal day would start with an hour of yoga. The practice of yoga is key in our way of working. Apart from physical fitness, it warms up the body and enables the actors to be energetic throughout the day. It helps in body alignment and balance, which brings unity to the body system, directing the group's focus for the day. Dance warm-ups and routines would follow through theatre exercises and then work on the text. For all of us I must say it was more of a learning process since we incorporated the project with the six-week performance training programme that the company uses. It basically tackles the topics of the actor, use of voice in speech, music, percussion, characterization, devising work and also working with the text, which was reworked as a mixture of English and Swahili. We learned in the best and most fun way we could.

Growing up as a young girl from the Bukusu community in the Western part of Kenya, my grandmother would use proverbs (*mafumbo*) to teach me about life lessons. Relating to how Wole Soyinka wrote *The Lion and the Jewel* always reminded me of my roots and grandmother when I heard:

> ...aaah! Ailatu that was gentle, be sweet and sharp
> like the swift sting of a wasp for there lies the pleasure[1]

– to describe the notion of grabbing opportunities while they are presented to you there and then. The depth and passion of the characters and the beautifully and richly crafted language was a constant motivation as it was also a challenge since you have to constantly read the play over and over to understand the actual intent of the writer and to get the feel and flow of the whole story. I found *The Lion and the Jewel* an exciting musical, full of drama, thrills, varied emotions and tempo, and just bringing all these to life through songs, dance and the words themselves was a rewarding process. Having to discover deeper meanings regarding what the characters tell each other, and helping my actors understand the play was another highlight for me.

Since we were doing it in Mombasa, we decided to change the setting to Kenya, specifically the Coast so that the audience would relate to it and also to constantly remind ourselves about the story that Wole Soyinka wants to tell. First of all, we changed the Ibo words in the text to Giriama/Swahili. Words like Ilujinle changed to Kadzandani, Lion (only where it is used to refer to Baroka) to Simba, Okiki to Gumbao, among others. Most of the actors had difficulty in understanding the text, as most of us are more the Lakunle 'type', who think we are 'polished and civilized'. Most of us, if not all, claim to be westernized just because we've attended school to university level or got lucky to study abroad unlike our grandparents. The reality is we are confused and stuck and, if moving, definitely in the wrong direction because we still feel empty because we are not close to being western in mannerism and character yet we have drifted apart from our cultures and traditions in as much as we have gained the degrees. The scene where the village girls come to inform Sidi of her pictures taken by the stranger and now spread in a magazine was a perfect fit since Mombasa is not only known for good food but also great gossip. I decided on the use of pure Swahili with a few extra words complete with the physical expression of the body and not forgetting their high-pitched voices! To quote one of my favourite parts:

> Village girl 1: *Sidi! Kuna picha moja umepigwa kutoka utosini hadi …*
> Village girl 2: *Viganjani*
> Village girl 1: *Nakwaambia umenyoosha mkono utafikiri jua lilikua ni mpenzi Chunare wako…haha! Naye Baroka amefichwa kwenye kona na la chakuchekesha ni kwamba yuasaidiana na choo la kijiji!* [2]

When it was performed, all the audience members got really excited about it especially because most of them have said just those words, and they were just seeing a reflection of themselves in the mirror of the performance.

The costumes used in our performances were *lesos* and *kikois*, a coastal culture of dressing where the rectangular shaped, coloured pieces of cloth are decorated with words that have different messages, for example, '*Pili pili imepandwa shambani, mjini yakuashiani?*' (Hot pepper grown in the rural area, why does it make you sneeze in the city?) This one is a message to people who love poking their noses in other people's businesses. Such proverbs were used to constantly remind the audience of the setting.

All the flashback scenes were choreographed into a dance with the actors singing Giriama songs to add texture and layers to the overall picture of the story. Giriama is one of the nine sub-groups under the Mijikenda people of the Kenyan Coast. We used a Giriama work-song to add to the construction of the railway scene. We also used two West African songs that enhanced the dances and were also a way to acknowledge where the whole inspiration of the play comes from.

The performance took place on 14 and 15 December 2013 at the Little Theatre's Amphitheatre. Since the story unfolds in a day, the timings were just perfect: when it was getting dark, the play was also getting into the night scene. The kind of setting used was a live setting, with the headlights of a car giving the rural and serene feel completed with candles stuck into the ground with sand and covered with coloured paper 'lanterns'. When darkness came we had people watching the play from the balconies of their apartments which overlook the theatre, providing an urban setting with an actual wall separating us from them. The actors easily felt the space and the progress of the day since it was happening there and then. Nature worked to our advantage and the actors lived the moments of the characters they played.

For most of the actors, this was their first theatre performance and it was really exciting for both them and myself. I have worked with them before as their trainer and watching them grow the same way others have watched me grow was a priceless gift.

The coastal culture itself has beliefs and traditional practices that Soyinka's play allowed the audience members to relate to and live through again. The shift from the West African to the Mombasa setting I would say was well received by the audience. I imagine we achieved this by drawing on the two different energies of the East and West; the colourful, dreamy, gossip-filled, Mombasa energy and the more aggressive, over the top Nigerian style.

NOTES

1   This is not a direct quote from Soyinka as the play was adapted by the current writer.
2   Translates into English as:
    Village girl 1: Sidi! There is one photo where you have been photographed from the forehead to....
    Village girl 2: Hands
    Village girl 1: I tell you you have stretched your hand, one would think the sun was your lover. Poor you.
    (Laughter) And Baroka has been hidden in a corner. And the funny thing is that it's near the village toilet!

Encounters with Ngũgĩ

I
Choru wa Mũirũrĩ
Reflections on the Kamĩrĩĩthũ experience

MUGO MUHIA

Choru wa Mũirũrĩ was born 62 years ago in Kamaandũra – a village near Kamĩrĩĩthũ – but grew up in Kamĩrĩĩthũ itself, where his father, a settler's cook, stationed his young family during the period of independence agitation in a concentration village which had been established by the then colonial administration in its effort at quashing the Mau Mau rebellion. He started his primary education at Lĩmuru Mission Primary, then called Holy Ghost Missionary and proceeded to Ngenia High School for his O-level education.

Kamĩrĩĩthũ Community and Education Centre was established in 1976. Its main agenda was improvement of literacy in Kamĩrĩĩthũ and its environs and its key targets were the adults and elderly who did not have a basic education. As an educated member of Kamĩrĩĩthũ community, Choru was requested to assist in teaching as a volunteer at the centre and he readily agreed. He started teaching Language at the elementary level to the elderly learners. He states his teaching methodology was dictated by the memory he had of how his teachers used to teach them as he was not a trained teacher himself.

It was while at the Centre that the idea of theatre was introduced to him, and he claims that he had no prior experience in theatre or drama. Ngũgĩ wa Mĩriĩ, his age mate and school mate, joined Kamĩrĩĩthũ as a researcher from the University of Nairobi's Department of Education and Extra-Mural Studies, in adult education and literacy. When Ngũgĩ wa Thiong'o came, the Centre had already formed various committees which had been charged with helping the management run the Centre, and the question of what could be done to make the Centre more useful to the community had already been raised. After some persuasion Ngũgĩ wa Thiong'o agreed to write the play that finally emerged as *Ngaahika Ndeenda / I Will Marry When I Want*. The title resonated well with the people as this was taken from the then popular song by D.K. wa Wanja with the same title.

Choru, as a volunteer teacher and member of the committee, was amongst the first people to read the script. The number of people who wanted take part were so many that most roles were given to more than one actor. The issues that the play raised were based on the actors' real live experiences and so the relationship between reality and fiction was collapsed. He gives examples of men and women who had taken part in the struggle for independence reliving the pains of betrayal, while the wounds of their experience in the same were quite visible: women with partial fingers, limping men, those on crutches etc. He claims that some did not even need the playwright's words: they would re-enact the reality of their experiences on stage using their own words. One of the play's protagonists, Gĩcaamba (Kamau wa Wakaba) and his co-actor (Karanja wa Fred), were actually workers at the Bata Shoe company and the sounding of the siren on stage mirrored the reality of their day-to-day working experience. Some of the characters were so real that one of the directors had to remind them that this was a play, not reality, and sometimes the audience's hatred of characters like Ikuua was visible.

For his part, Choru says that his appreciation of the play mingled with the little he had read about the state of the working class globally, the political debate between East and West Germany, the Cold War, etc., and so when the play is coming to the end and the trumpet is sounded calling for the workers of the world to arise in unity and oneness, it aroused in him a passion and a conviction that things can change for the better if only people agree to join hands. This was in spite of the fact that he played Kĩoi, the rich land owner, who is not appreciated by the audience as some would insult him from where they sat.

But Choru confesses that he loved acting Kĩoi. To him there was nothing wrong with riches; what is wrong is the manner in which they are achieved and how one uses them in relations with others. He recalls with nostalgia walking around the stage with a walking stick and a suit, and an exaggerated walking style befitting his status: "I could see a sense of admiration from the audience … and well … for the few minutes I acted I enjoyed that world", but this was with a little sense of regret as if bemoaning that momentary status of riches that was never to be. He recalls the reaction of the audience when they were at one time acting *Ngaahika Ndeenda/ I Will Marry When I Want* in Kerũgoya and they were so angry with Ikuua (Mũturi) that they threw their shoes at him and insulted him, and when the play ended and it came to entertainment the locals refused to buy Mũturi any drinks. The play continued to elicit a lot of passion, especially in many parts of Central Kenya.

Choru explains that the sustained passion that the play continued to elicit was, he thought, based on the one hand on the people's historical recollection of the Mau Mau struggle and the significance of the names. This kind of naming helped audiences see the characters' true self embedded both in their actions and personality. A character like Ndugĩre was a replica of 'Kunda ngũtũme', a colonial collaborator, and their existence was [so] visible throughout Kamĩrĩĩthũ and its surroundings that people needed little evidence to unmask their true identity even on the stage and could even pinpoint them in the society. These names had meaning beyond their immediate use.

Choru wa Mũirũri: Reflections on Kamĩrĩĩthũ 39

While it is true that the two Ngũgĩs brought the script – the reworking of the songs and dances, the movements and the general aesthetics of the play were added by the people. It was simply a communal affair: a community dealing with their historical and daily experiences on stage with freedom to frame them according to how they lived then. Choru says that Ngũgĩ wa Thiong'o never interfered with the rehearsals but was always scribbling things in his notebook, especially when characters deviated from the script, but when a chance to make a particular decision came, he always carried the day. Choru thinks that the whole community theatre project must have been lying in Ngũgĩ's mind or was already a prepared project and that Kamĩrĩĩthũ only provided a springboard for the maturation of his ideas. He therefore credits the success of the whole project to Ngũgĩ wa Thiong'o, but not to his age mate and school mate, Ngũgĩ wa Mĩriĩ:

> [With] the banning of the play and the subsequent detention of one of its authors, a hush fell across the Kamĩrĩĩthũ community, and there was palpable anger and defiance but the presence of armed policemen at the centre was so glaring a reminder of what the force of arms could do to unarmed populace, [that] the reality of their fate during the struggle for independence stood like indelible marks on their bodies: reluctantly the cast started breaking apart but the rumours (*mĩhehũ*) of how things should have been continued instilling a willingness and courage to do it again if called.

The fate of Kamĩrĩĩthũ Cultural and Education Centre is a part of the Kenyan tragedy, a travesty of justice and an example of how far a despotic regime can go in silencing the people. It has become a historical narrative and societies in Africa and elsewhere have taken it further. The physical burning of the Centre brings strains and hurt both on Choru's forehead and in his eyes, albeit momentarily: it was to take eleven long years for the group to revive the Kamĩrĩĩthũ dream under a new name of Kamĩrĩĩthũ Cultural Troupe, spearheaded by Choru and Nyambura wa Ngũgĩ in 1993. It was easy to summon the majority of the original cast as the roles had been done [by] two or more people each.

We staged *Ngaahika Ndeenda/I Will Marry When I Want* at the Kikuyu Country Club and the proprietor Njoroge wa Gathĩnji was really instrumental in organizing the performances. The underlying willingness to restage the play was because of the wind of multi-party politics that was blowing across the Kenyan nation, making the group think that the time was now ripe for the revival of the Kamĩrĩĩthũ theatre. But little did they know that there was a silent rule still in place, especially in the whole hierarchy of security administration: from chiefs, District Officers, District Commissioners and Provincial Commissioners, concerning Ngũgĩ wa Thiong'o and his theatrical activities. Even when these offices readily gave them the licence to act the play, the performances were always stopped at the beginning after singing the national anthem or mid-way. This happened in Kikuyu, Kĩambu and Nakuru.

With time, the government slowly relaxed its clamp-down on the group's activities and the performances started going on without undue interference. Kamĩrĩĩthũ Cultural Troupe started staging *I Will Marry* at Sports View Hotel Kasarani, Nairobi which they did from the beginning of 1994 during weekends for about three months. During Easter of the same year they took the play to Mombasa's Leisure Village, where they partnered with the owner. He offered them accommodation and food while they did the shows, but the timing was wrong because their target audience was the Kikuyu, and as most had travelled upcountry for the holidays, the number of people who came to watch was quite low.

They travelled widely, covering parts of Kīambu: Kikuyu Country Club, Kiboko Hotel, Līmuru, Red Nova, Kīambu Town; Keroguya, Embu: Isaac Walton Hotel, and Nakuru at the Railways Club and Rift Valley Sports Club. Choru gives an experience in Nakuru when the play was stopped at the Railways Club and the cast with the help of members of the audience organized an alternative venue at the Rift Valley Sports Club. By the time the authorities knew what was happening the play had gone well past the middle. The D.O. of the area, a Mr Mwaūra, came and requested them to stop as he feared for his job even though he did not see any harm in watching the play. The reception was always sizable and in some places like Kerūgoya they were requested to repeat performances on Sunday. This time they had started including *Maitū Njugīra/ Mother Sing for Me* as part of the performance.

During all this time, Choru was working in Mombasa and would travel so as to join the cast and travel back to Mombasa on Sunday night. To him even when he did not get any material rewards, the satisfaction that came with the performances was a reward in itself. He spent a lot of his money in funding some of the group's activities like travel and food. But there were times when particular individuals would invite them to go and act, like when a magistrate by the name of Mr Gīthīnji invited them to Machakos and paid all their expenses. In most of the places they went, the audience was predominantly Kikuyu. He explains this as a concretization of the then opposition politics which was the form of political identity that the community had coalesced around. They therefore identified with the resistance and opposition themes which are central in the two plays.

Redirecting the plays under these circumstances was a strenuous affair even though they did not add anything new. Sometimes the songs would be reworded, tunes changed and movements changed. Choru also recalls the disappointment on reading in the media of a reporter who referred to him as an amateur director whose cast did their best, not because of his good directing or input but out love/respect for him. He was hurt because the said reporter did not know the challenges they had had to overcome before restaging the plays.

One of the lessons that Choru learned from taking part in the plays was the importance of the community to the life of the individual. The Kamīrīīthū successes were an effort of many hands working together to make their lives meaningful. Whether these indeed transformed the individual members is a story of another day. He also learnt about the need of families to reason together before making a decision without allowing outside influence over the decisions they make: this he thinks is the tragedy of Kīguunda's family, it is good to listen to people's opinions and advice but in the end we must make the most favourable decision that benefits the family. He also learnt about the importance of courage, the importance of defending our rights as human beings, the role of leaders in any society and the centrality of resistance as the pathway to communal and individual emancipation.

The plays remain relevant today as they were then because the same things that convinced us to act are still in place today. Young people are still unemployed, only that today they are better educated than we were. Most of them, especially from financially unstable families, find it very hard to get jobs and end up working as manual labourers. Around them, they can see children from rich and politically connected families getting better jobs even though in school they might have been academically weaker. If somebody was to come up with another project like Kamĩrĩĩthũ, these young people would have similar conviction and agency we had, because the reality of their lives is still much the same as ours thirty-seven years ago. The enduring warning etched in the plays is that society, and especially the government of the day, must put up measures to mitigate the despair that continues [to] eat our nation's citizenry or risk massive resistance.

Well, it is 8 p.m. at night and I must travel back to Nairobi. Choru has to go back home to entertain his grand children, the children of his eldest daughter, who had been nick-named '*maitũ njugĩra*'/ Waruthu wa Mũirũrĩ.

Interview by Mũgo Mũhĩa 12 April 2014, B2 Bar and Restaurant, Lĩmuru.

II
Producing *I Will Marry When I Want* in South Africa

FREDERICK MBOGO

From casual conversations that I had had with a variety of theatre practitioners in Nairobi, I had gathered that Ngũgĩ wa Thiong'o's plays were extremely difficult, if not impossible, to stage. Their main problem was the huge cast required to give life to the many characters in them. How can a theatre practitioner anywhere in the world, mostly working with minimum funding, hope to stage a work so demanding without collapsing? A huge cast requires many hours of rehearsing, an expensive wardrobe, managerial stress from the massaging of the numerous actors' and actresses' egos, and a suitable venue for the eventual staging of the work. Add to these problems the very nature of a Nairobi audience that has since the early 1990s been nurtured on theatre work that is constantly oscillating between slapstick comedy and farces by British writers that entwine salacious attitudes with witty dialogue. Never mind that Ngũgĩ wa Thiong'o is a renowned writer, so the conversations went, the average Kenyan theatre-goer has no respect for 'serious' drama. Sadly, this thoughtline still permeates the psyche of the Kenyan theatre practitioner until, sometimes some donor or other comes along, funds a project or two and disappears.

In 2003, Professor Malcolm Purkey of the University of Witwatersrand asked me to consider staging any play by a major African writer at the Wits Amphitheatre in Johannesburg, South Africa, where I was about to graduate with a Masters Degree in Dramatic Arts. I was seduced immediately by the idea of working on Wole Soyinka's *Death and the King's Horseman* which I admired immensely. But there was this constant niggling within me to try out something risqué, a troublesome play. I thought I needed an unfinished play or at least one that would engage me in a way that wasn't usual for a director. *Death and the King's Horseman*, is technically a well 'finished' play whose characters face interesting choices but whose fates are tied, sometimes, to forces beyond them. That was exciting enough, yet in my directorial mind I felt I needed a play that had a possibility of action from the characters' point of view – without some external force pushing them into action. This internal debate was interesting as it took me through readings of works by a multitude of writers. Well, I stopped at Ngũgĩ wa Thiong'o and Ngũgĩ wa Mĩriĩ's *I Will Marry When I Want*, possibly because I had read about it in Ngũgĩ wa Thiong'o's *Decolonising the Mind* and had romanticized its coming to being through the mobilization of people power at Kamĩrĩĩthũ. Besides, the need to respond to the voices in earlier conversations with theatre practitioners on the place of Ngũgĩ wa Thiong'o's plays came calling. Of course, there was also a feeling that I was going to deal with the familiar in an unfamiliar fashion – putting the Kenya of *I Will Marry When I Want* to a South African audience whose realities might be different.

My first problem after settling for *I Will Marry When I Want* was how to cast the play. I was working within the University of Witwatersrand's main campus in Johannesburg, therefore it was relatively easy to pin up posters calling for auditions. Yet, the first question that arose from many who came for the auditions was stark: 'Are you recruiting blacks only?' Well, I had not thought about that, at least not in the way it was asked. I felt uncomfortable given that in Kenya, where I had staged many plays before, I hadn't come across a race question of this nature. But these questions also made me recall all that I had read about apartheid, so that I shuddered to imagine a labelling of the play as a 'blacks only' theatre work. How could I be so insensitive? But how was I to work with white actors in a play set around Kamĩrĩĩthũ where the people were still reeling from effects of colonial oppression?

I was worried that by not allowing white actors in my play I would be accused of practising the very same racism that was the main thread in apartheid. At some point I closed my eyes and came to a conclusion; I must be true to the spirit of the play which is not necessarily racist but speaks a certain truth about race relations. I decided to go with the 'fact' that the play is about a certain people whose world view is necessarily black, if there can be such! The discomfort never left me, though.

I had decided that the running time of the play would be limited to seventy minutes without any interval. The play, as published, should last at least two hours. That meant that parts of the play had to be cut out which was a painful process. The idea was to remain with the spine of the story and a through line, as Constantin Stanislavski would say, that suggests the play's main interest. Minor characters were affected in this so that Njooki, for example, who is Gĩcaamba's wife in the play, had parts of her speeches reduced. On the other hand, Gĩcaamba, who is a main character with what sometimes seem to be endless monologues is made to say only that which adds to the through line.

While the play's main idea is to discuss the problems of the peasantry and workers in a horribly capitalist post-colonial Kenya, it does have other serious aspects that affirm the culture of a people. There is for instance an elaborate replay (flashback) of a 'traditional' Gĩkũyũ wedding between Kĩgũũnda, a farm labourer and Wangeci, his lover, complete with songs and local dances. The importance of this wedding in the play is that it is contrasted with another that is not 'traditional' but following in the tenets of the Christian church. This helps to show that weddings are employed as cultural instruments by the oppressor, who has brought Christianity to be consumed as a sedative by the oppressed.

The peasantry and working class becomes blinded to the land grab, overwork, underpay and inhumane conditions of their living wrought by the conspiring of the owners of capital and the governors of the land, through the tranquilizing power of the Church. Yet, for the practical interest of maintaining the seventy-minute running time, not everything could be brought to life. The 'traditional' wedding was not therefore elaborately enacted while the Christian wedding, which is imagined in a conversation between Kīgūūnda and his wife, is only given space as part of a mockery of the Church's practices – for instance, the white dress for the bride suggests that she is pure, and virgin. This cutting and reducing of speeches and statements was difficult because it meant that certain meanings would be lost and new ones possibly brought to light.

The practical engagements during rehearsals would sometimes shape the 'final' script on stage. One particular case involved an actress, Juannita Azannai, who was playing Jezebel, Kīoi's wife. Although she was playing a minor character, she played her part with such dexterity as she explored the delicate art of hypocrisy that she became difficult to ignore. It was possible to employ her character as the major instrument in the play's exploration of how Christianity was bent to accommodate the interests of the oppressors. Jezebel, being Kīoi's wife, is tasked with the idea of protecting the property of her husband through preaching the virtues of Christianity. Her husband is a wealthy man who is a farmer and businessman employing many ordinary people. He is therefore involved in the many acts of exploitation and acquisitions of land that may be deemed exploitative. Kīgūūnda, the farm labourer, is meant to be his victim but he is resistant. Jezebel is the gifted wife who cajoles the Kīgūūndas to accept the deal on offer, selling their small plot of land which is their only security. She attempts to convince them to solemnize their marriage in a Christian way and suggests that she will help them in any way to achieve the dream of marrying in such a 'civilized' fashion. But her hypocritical stance is seen in the subtle ways that she treats the Kīgūūndas when they come to her house.

She cringes from their heathenness in a physical sense by making them occupy the 'worst' seats in her house. She also seems to want to disinfect everything that they touch. Jezebel's character is modelled from the Jezebel of the Bible who is the wife of King Ahab. In the Bible she is said to have misdirected the people towards declaring a landowner guilty of blasphemy, among other evils, and therefore inciting the killing of an innocent man. In the play, Jezebel becomes the soft power who employs religion to cheat landowners to give in to the wiles of Kīoi, her husband, whose need is to acquire property in any way possible.

Weaving this story so that it is brought to life to illustrate the essentials of life for the peasantry and workers was always going to be difficult but had to be done. The trick was to balance the main issues and the practical needs of the play in terms of time and also the management of the many characters.

But there was also the problem of ideas; what was the relevance of *I Will Marry When I Want* to a South Africa where the key issues differ from those of Kenya? How was this play to be made to respond to urgent questions that

South Africans have about themselves? There was a risk, I thought, of this play appearing as though it were a piece that captures a glorious afternoon in the lives of peasants somewhere in Kenya. In other words, the play could be used by students of history, or archeology and even literature, as merely a work that is a mobile, speaking museum. Granted, issues in the play do appear once in a while in life: hypocrisy, exploitation, loss of innocence, culture, and identity, but what would be the immediacy of this to my audience? As I agonized over this, COSATU (Congress of South African Trade Unions) started a series of meetings that culminated in a strike that was dubbed by parts of South African media as 'South Africa's biggest strike' – as *The Star* of 16 September 2004 reported, for example. The strike then made the play a relevant one as it brought to the fore issues that workers have against the owners of capital. Indeed, the question of land ownership and rights to production came alongside the strike as a sticking question to a regime that had vowed to serve all equally.

In a sense, therefore, the play was somewhat prophetic of events that would come to haunt South African people. It suggested that two differing 'worlds', Kenya and South Africa, can have a common destiny as their problems are similar. But I felt that there were still some niggling questions: can there be a neo-Marxism that reimagines the place of the worker as a liberator who hasn't been seduced by capitalism? Is there hope that capital will one day land in the hands of a more humane cadre of capitalists or are we merely fantasizing that one day life will be sweet for the oppressed and oppressor alike?

There were interesting problems during rehearsals, especially as regards pronounciation of names. The cast was largely from Southern Africa, so much so that 'Wangeci' was pronounced as 'Wang'enthi', at first. But the most fascinating aspect of the play to the cast was the revelation of the story behind the play. The narrative of how Ngũgĩ was contacted by a woman from Kamĩrĩĩthũ so that an initiative was created that led to the creation of the play resonated with some of the actors playing major parts. Jeremiah Ntonga, playing Kĩgũũnda for instance, could now come to terms with his first lines: 'These one and a half acres? These are worth more to me than all the thousands that belong to Ahab Kĩoi wa Kanoru. These are my own, not borrowed robes said to tire the wearer. A man brags about his own penis. However tiny.' The idea that land can be likened to a very private aspect of the human body was of major interest. It brought to the fore central questions about land that may have easily escaped the largely urban cast of this play to whom land as a resource might at first have seemed like a remote idea.

The songs employed in the play were always going to be of interest. We employed both Kiswahili songs picked from choruses that are sung in church and songs of protest from South Africa. They had to make meaning for the viewers but we started with reinterpreting them for our specific purposes. They had to be songs that could easily enable visual aspects such as dance and which had to be backed by drumming or other instrumentation. One particular Kiswahili song, picked from a church chorus, was '*Shetani akija*' (When the Devil comes). It has a militaristic sound to it and can be turned into a marching band tune. Its beauty lies in the actions that the singers make in preparing themselves to fight the Devil. The song suggests that the Devil should be crushed under foot when he comes near you (*akija pande yako, kanyaga kanyaga kanyaga*) (when he comes to your side, step on him, crush him and crush him again). The song was sung in the first scene at Kīgūūnda's yard where the writers have suggested a hymn entitled: 'The Satan of poverty must be crushed'. It has the same undertones and serves an interesting purpose which brought out various interpretations during our rehearsals. In what sense, the actors wanted to know, is religion so powerful as to permeate the minds of the workers to such an extent? I tried to argue that perhaps the place of religion is more in the direction of providing some sort of therapy for the workers from the harsh conditions of their lives. Kīgūūnda is sympathetic to Kamande wa Munyui who has just passed by the house singing in a drunken state. His therapy seems to be alcohol. Similarly when the church group comes into Kīgūūnda's yard, they are likened to the intoxicated Munyui, who must take alcohol for survival. They must partake in religious acts for their survival too, which is as sorry a thing as being alcohol dependant. It is religion not for its own sake or some honest worship but as an escape from mental anguish.

Perhaps the most illuminating aspect of the interpretation of the play by the cast was their need to express what they thought was the most appropriate way to end the performance. This was in the Zulu language song that was selected to be sung last. It was a version of the popular '*Awulethu umshini wam*' (Bring my machine gun). It has in recent times been employed by supporters of Jacob Zuma when facing accusations of rape (2005/2006), so that it has had connotations that have been sexual – with '*Umdzidzi wam*' (Bring back my buttocks), being one of the adaptations. But in 2004, the song was still an important tool in the rememorization of *Umkhonto We Sizwe's* (The Spear of the Nation – the military wing of the ANC) fighting of the apartheid system. It has also been employed by mine workers in their numerous strikes. The song's call is to fight against oppression. Its use in the play's last scene projected a hopeful ending where the peasant and worker are made to imagine that they can be determiners of their own existence. It's a call for revolution through destroying those symbols that represent capitalists and their need to oppress. The song was used instead of the writers' suggested 'The trumpet of the worker has been blown'.

The play ran from the 27th of September to the 9th of October 2004. There was an audience for each of the days that we staged the play at the Wits Amphitheatre. However, on the first day of performance we had a 'special' audience. On the 5th of October, there was a specific 'Kenyan' night where the ambassador of Kenya to South Africa attended. These two sets of audiences were interesting, firstly because of their views on land issues. The South Africans seemed to appreciate the precarious state of land given that Zimbabwe, under Robert Mugabe, had decided to go on the route of forceful acquisition of land from former white owners. The Kenyans on the other hand, at least from the ambassador's point of view, felt scandalized by the play that seemed to be taking them back to days they did not want to re-experience. The problem, for the Kenyans, was that there was now a new government in place under Mwai Kibaki which had been voted in through some sort of euphoria that felt the need to do away with President Daniel arap Moi. How then could we go back to castigating government and showcasing capitalist exploitation as a Kenyan way of thinking? Suffice to say, the thought was that the play was not a true reflection of Kenya's current intents.

But there were also other Kenyans who thought the play spoke about a problem that must not be swept under the carpet. Land remains a serious issue as has been shown through the violence that exploded in 2007/2008 and which has been partly blamed on historical injustices. The South Africans also appreciated the questioning of how free one becomes after attaining some form of political empowerment. The issues of economic exploitation and the imbalance that there is between wealth creators or wielders of key resources against those who are the workers who create the resources was appreciated. There were conversations after the play that suggested that this was a major question that was facing South Africa. In that light then, one can argue that the play's intention of questioning the status quo was well achieved. It refused to merely be an antiquated piece of museum art.

III
Ngũgĩ wa Thiong'o
The unrecognized Black Hermit

OBY OBYERODHYAMBO

One could easily argue that Ngũgĩ is one of Kenya's most significant cultural exports. Over half a century, he has penned celebrated plays, novels, essays and has been fêted all over the world. His books are translated into over thirty languages. Ngũgĩ wa Thiong'o has been honoured with countless awards as well as honorary doctorate degrees. In his motherland, he remains the proverbial unaccepted prophet. His detention and subsequent flight from Kenya to escape political persecution made him more famous, or infamous. At the height of the political intolerance of Moi's autocratic regime, Ngũgĩ was a pariah in his homeland. Many of his works had been banned by the government of the day, with novels that had for a long while been English literature set-books in high school, like *The River Between* and *A Grain of Wheat*, pulled out of the national school curriculum. Following the razing to the ground of his Limuru based Kamĩrĩĩthũ Theatre, associated with his plays *I Will Marry When I Want* (*Ngahiika Ndeenda*) and *Mother Sing for Me* (*Maitũ Njugĩra*), producers actively avoided his plays. The state's displeasure with Ngũgĩ and his writing was obvious and the intimidation of those who tried to revive the 'spirit' of Ngũgĩ or that of Kamĩrĩĩthũ was loud and clear: one produced an Ngũgĩ play at one's own risk.

In 1988, the Daniel arap Moi regime supported national celebrations all over Kenya to mark ten years of the president's rule; an enterprise that was dubbed The Nyayo Era Celebrations. The Free Travelling Theatre of the University of Nairobi with which Ngũgĩ had been associated at its inception chose to perform Wole Soyinka's *Kongi's Harvest* under the direction of Gachũgũ Makini. Makini had been a cast member in the 1977 World Black Festival of Arts and Culture (FESTAC) production of *The Trial of Dedan Kĩmathi*, and was also involved in the *Maitũ Njugĩra* production. The irony of this choice was lost on the organizing committee of the celebrations until someone from the Literature Department at the University of Nairobi pointed it out. The show was a satirical mockery of what had popularly gained the moniker, *Nyayo Errors*. The national celebration committee allegedly demanded an explanation as to why the university troupe had chosen a '*foreign*' play to be mounted during celebration of a uniquely Kenyan event. As a result, the Vice Chancellor of the University of Nairobi, Phillip Mbithi, decided to cancel this particular contribution to the celebrations, but allowed the *Kongi's Harvest* performance to go ahead the week after the *Nyayo Error* celebrations. This was self-censorship at its worst, a regular occurrence at the University at the time. Piqued by this decision, the cast, under the banner of Theatre Workshop Productions, decided to retaliate. The challenge had been to perform a Kenyan play. We dropped all subtleties and made a decision to stage a Kenyan play by a Kenyan author: *The Trial of Dedan Kīmathi* by Ngũgĩ wa Thiong'o and Mīcere Mūgo.

The Trial of Dedan Kīmathi had not been performed in Kenya since the detention and exile of the author for fear of reprisal from the authorities. For this reason, the 1990 production was legendary. The very contemplation by the cast of mounting a Ngũgĩ play was momentous and symbolic. Following the purchase of the scripts, the reading of the play was an attempt at re-creating the mood of the 1977 production where Ngũgĩ and the cast rehearsed the play in the University of Nairobi's Education Theatre II. The story of the controversy surrounding attempts to perform *The Trial of Dedan Kīmathi* at the Kenya National Theatre in 1977 before the group left for the FESTAC event in Lagos is a well-documented milestone in the history of Kenyan theatre, described elsewhere thus:

> ...more important were the controversial pre-festival productions, which took place in the Kenya National Theatre between October 20 and 30, 1976. So successful were the performances that the audiences spilled into the streets each night chanting the politically explosive songs in the play. (Raji: 2009, 42)

The Theatre Workshop Productions (TWP) cast set about the first euphoric and daunting task of learning the Mau Mau songs. It is important to note that it was not until the Kibaki presidency (2002-13) that Mau Mau was unproscribed and as such the Mau Mau songs were actually *illegal anthems* even in the 1990s. Unlike the original Ngũgĩ production where there must have been creative 'consultants' who had actually sung these war songs in the forest on the slopes of Mt Kenya this cast had no such luxury. It took creative ingenuity to seek out individual actors familiar with the songs to act as teachers not just of the tunes, but the nuances of lyrics and performance or delivery styles. The Mau Mau songs were created in a war situation as rallying calls for the fighters and their supporters and thus are laden with symbolism and *double entendre*. The multi-ethnic cast had to pore through the songs in the original Gīkūyū language explicating each, and critically analysing every song to decipher the meanings as envisaged by the Mau Mau. The collection of Mau Mau songs and poetry by Maina wa Kīnyatti[1] served as an excellent resource. The collection gave the cast an authentic feel of the fighter's operational context, their ideological commitment to the cause they were fighting for and their creative genius.

Field Marshall Dedan Kīmathi occupies a highly contested mythological status in Kenya. He was a commander of the Kenya Land and Freedom Army (KLFA) and the leader of the Mau Mau movement. He was captured by the British, convicted in a kangaroo trial, executed, and buried in a secret grave.

Though there is national recognition of the role played by the Mau Mau in the liberation struggle, its leader's place in history is at best ambivalent. Unofficially, Dedan Kīmathi is a martyr of the liberation war, but officially the Kenyatta and Moi regimes refused to accord him or his army special historical recognition. The national discomfiture with the role of the Mau Mau in the struggle for independence in Kenya is central to the play bearing his name. The play argues that independence was hijacked by those who did not participate in the struggle to liberate the country. It described the ruling elite as the progeny of the '*homeguards*'[1] and *tie-tie*.[2] This depiction was consistent with the Fanonist-Marxist dialectic that Ngũgĩ and Mĩcere Mũgo had imbued in the character of Kīmathi. As the *de facto* dramaturg for the production, this writer questioned whether Ngũgĩ, in making Kīmathi sound very dialectic actually alienated him from the masses, ordinary people who would have been moved by his rhetoric. The length and denseness of the Kīmathi diatribes made him appear a demagogue rather than the charismatic leader that he is famed to have been. The script fails to capture the eloquence of his speeches as he addresses his comrades in arms. In the 1990 production, therefore, a fair amount of lines meant for Kīmathi were deleted, and some shared out among the other Generals[3] whose roles had previously been minimal. The production took the decision to create a more collegiate leader as opposed to an autocratic one. The group also found it inaccurate and disturbing that the play did not provide for a female among the generals when historically there are recorded the narratives of generals such as Mũthoni who fought in the war. Their active presence in a dramatic text such as this one would have corroborated the role and location of women in the struggle for independence. Since it would have been too great a departure from the scripts TWP resisted the temptation to make one of the generals female.

A performance of *The Trial of Dedan Kīmathi* in 1990 should have been a celebration of a national hero, but the production was threatened with denial of 'permission' to go on stage just as Ngũgĩ wa Thiong'o and Mĩcere Mũgo had been in 1977. The university administration was jittery, fearing the official perception by the Moi regime of the sanctioning of a play by the exiled duo, Ngũgĩ wa Thiong'o and Mĩcere Mũgo, that celebrated their arch-nemesis. The production team was apprehensive that at the last minute the university administration would manufacture an excuse to stop the performance.

Salvation for *The Trial of Dedan Kīmathi* came from the most unexpected of quarters. Nelson Mandela, who had been released from prison, was making an African tour to thank the African nations that had stood by the ANC in its struggle, and among the countries he visited was Kenya. In his speech to thousands of ecstatic Kenyans at Kasarani, he paid glowing homage to the heroes of Kenya's liberation struggle, describing them as having been an inspiration to his struggle. He mentioned Jomo Kenyatta and noted that he had been honoured by the act of laying a wreath at his mausoleum. He then mentioned Dedan Kīmathi and the crowd went wild. He noted that Kīmathi was as much a hero of the struggle for freedom in South Africa as he was in Kenya. Mandela went on to make the point that he regretted that there was no grave at which he could have paid homage. As if this was not telling enough he added that he had regretfully learnt that Dedan Kīmathi's widow lived outside of Nairobi and although he would have loved to meet her and pay his respects this had not possible. He also spoke of General China, noting that although he was still alive, he too was beyond his reach outside Nairobi. Mandela then tasked the uncomfortable looking President Moi with conveying his respects to these heroes. In our rehearsals we cheered, knowing that this level of acknowledgement had unlocked the performance impasse. No one would dare shut down the play honouring Kīmathi after Mandela had heaped such accolades on him. The next day one of the dailies carried the headline 'Mandela Heaps Praise on Kīmathi'. The choice of image for the publicity material for our production quickly became clear. We produced posters with images of Mandela and Kīmathi, superimposing on their faces the newspaper clipping. Mandela had elevated the production beyond reproach.

Unlike other leaders of popular revolutions like Fidel Castro, Che Guevara, Samora Machel, or even Nelson Mandela, Kīmathi did not survive his war and so there is little in the form of his speeches or writings that an author or actor can access to better understand the man in flesh and blood and assist in a realistic portrayal. Ngũgĩ and Mīcere in their creation of Kīmathi sought to maintain this mythical figure while also trying to humanize him by showing doubts that plagued him. Portraying such a character as a believable human, yet at the same time a courageous military tactician to avoid a stereotypical rendition is a monumental challenge. Ngũgĩ and Mīcere Mūgo script a very one-dimensional character and in our production deliberations we were at pains to project a Kīmathi who was a husband, a father, an ex-teacher and performer, as well as a military leader. The mother of one of our cast members who had grown up in Ihũrũrũ, Karuna-inī, knew Dedan Kīmathi personally and had gone to school with him was an invaluable resource. Her description of him was of an ordinary man, a likeable man, one who would walk hand in hand with his partner on the hills and slopes of the land, yet one who was stung enough by the injustices of colonialism to take up armed struggle. The Kīmathi we wanted to play was one who reminded our audience of a favorite uncle whom we all love, who visits now and again and whose company we enjoy. The script does not give much leeway to humanize Kīmathi. Our Kīmathi was not one to instil the fear and awe that he supposedly evoked in the colonial administration to the extent that they killed him and secretly buried his body in an unmarked spot to avoid his grave turning into a sacred shrine to which people would have flocked to pay homage. We desired to liberate Kīmathi's spirit, raise him to the status of his peers, the African liberators, and perform as a symbol of the pride that we had indeed conquered the colonial forces. We did.

NOTES

1 '*Homeguards*' is a collective term that is used to describe the native population who sided with the colonial forces against the liberation fighters. Many such persons were rewarded with positions as colonial administrators and thus were able to send their children to school and eventually captured the state and sidelined the fighters.
2 *Tie-tie* was a term coined by the militant wing of Kenya African Union Association to refer to moderates: what amounts to an *African bourgeoisie* who loved to dress in ties.
3 Many of the Generals that Kīmathi fought with like Generals China, Baimunge and Matenjagwo Tumbo survived the war and offer a picture of Kīmathi that was more charismatic and less ideological.

WORKS CITED

Kīnyatti, Maina wa (1990), *Thunder From the Mountains: Mau Mau Patriotic Songs*. Trenton NJ: Africa World Press.
Raji, Wumi (2009), *Long Dreams in Short Chapters: Essays in African Postcolonial Literary, Cultural and Political Criticisms*. Berlin: LIT Verlag.

IV
Kamĩrĩĩthũ in Retrospect

GICHINGIRI NDIGIRIGI

In 'Kenyan Theatre after Kamĩrĩĩthũ' I argued that

> ...in its use of a local language as the medium of a major theatre production, Kamĩrĩĩthũ broke new ground. The effort at class-conscious theatre done by, for, and with the lower classes was also something new in Kenyan theatre. No intellectuals had been involved in this kind of effort before, nor has it been reproduced since. In relocating Kenyan theatre from the petty-bourgeois base at the institution of higher learning to the workers and peasants, Kamĩrĩĩthũ was also successful. (1999: 73)

I also provocatively stated that that Kamĩrĩĩthũ was a product unique to the 1970s and early 1980s in Kenya:

> Its effect on the Kenyan theatre scene was to a large extent dependent on Ngũgĩ and the intellectuals working with him, who were themselves products of the intellectual climate in the Kenya of the late 1970s and early 1980s. To the extent that Kamĩrĩĩthũ was successful, it also gave rise to conditions that made it difficult to reproduce its success. (*The Drama Review*, 1999:73)

A significant part of the article explored the obstacles presented by state censorship of theatre in the post-Kamĩrĩĩthũ phase, the dearth of theatre practitioners willing to take the kind of risks Ngũgĩ took with his art and life in the 1970s and '80s, and the overall commercialization of the theatre that ironically sucked in the performers from the radical Kamĩrĩĩthũ experiment of the 1970s. But much of that analysis was haunted by Ngũgĩ's consistent proclamation that Kamĩrĩĩthũ would one day come back. The end of Ngũgĩ's exile in 2004, his temporary return to Kenya, and the easing of state censorship calls for reflection on the successes of Kamĩrĩĩthũ and the lessons for the institutionalization of participatory theatre.

The official narrative of Kamĩrĩĩthũ has been told repeatedly in Ngũgĩ wa Thiong'o's writings. This version has been celebrated in African theatre scholarship that foregrounds the transformative nature of the Kamĩrĩĩthũ experiment in creating popular theatre. But, by and large, this narrative appears to privilege the accounts of the most visible participants by virtue of their academic positions. In this paper, I interject the multiple – and sometimes contradictory – perspectives of the other participants in the theatre projects. Drawing on extensive and probing open-ended interviews with a variety of the theatre participants, I draw out the lessons the Kamīrīīthū experience teaches with regard to the prospects of institutionalizing truly participatory theatre that would outlast topical concerns or the departure of a core group of participants. Several questions animate the discussion: to what extent was Kamīrīīthū truly dialogic? What impact did the events of 1977 and 1982 and the performances have on Ngũgĩ's life and art? How was the community affected by the theatre effort? If – as celebrated in the critical scholarship – Kamīrīīthū succeeded because of the presence of Ngũgĩ, a writer of international renown who was able to create reasonably professional scripts, to what extent would his greater – and continued – participation in the community have ensured the longevity of the theatre project? Paradoxically, then, to what extent was Kamīrīīthu dependent on a top-down model of social transformation? In sum, would there have been a Kamīrīīthu without Ngũgĩ?

One of the dimensions lauded in the Kamīrīīthū scholarship was its dialogic quality (Desai, 1990; Kerr, 1995; Kidd, 1983; and Brown, 1999). Desai particularly highlights the influence of Paulo Freire's ideas on dialogic education practice on the literacy project at Kamīrīīthū, an influence that allegedly seeped into the theatre project (1990: 83). While Kamīrīīthū looks like a cross between Brecht's 'theatre of instruction' and Augusto Boal's Forum Theatre with its problem-posing dialogue, and theatrical interventions that model solutions in the real world while breaking actor/spectator and teacher/student barriers, I want to suggest that the discussions during rehearsals were modelled on Socratic dialogues. Paul Dwyer raises an important question on Forum Theatre that is relevant to Kamīrīīthū when he asks: 'to what extent does a given dramaturgical modelling of a particular social problem bind us to discursive regimes which allow only certain ways of thinking about and carrying forward the process of social change?' (2004: 209).

In my interviews at Kamīrīīthu, I talked to many participants in both plays who give Ngũgĩ credit for his unobtrusiveness and his ability to listen, even to dissenting views. According to them, Ngũgĩ was never vocal or the first to speak in a discussion (Njũguna, Njaramba, Coru). But one perceptive participant noted that

> He is very good. You can talk to him. You will argue for a long time, but by the time he gives you an answer you might spend a whole day. He suggests this and that ... he twists this way and that, until he can really see that you have thought about the problem. Even by the time you get the answer, you are not even conscious of it. Yes, you cannot ask him a question and you get a direct answer. You have to sweat first.'
> (Gĩthiga Mwaũra, 20 February 1995)

Throughout the Kamīrīthū project, the villagers were collectively sweating for answers. But we have to remember that in his dialogues with Diogenes, Socrates suggested answers through the questions he posed, and this was the approach Ngũgĩ took with those who went to him for ready answers. Again and again, participants at Kamīrīīthū would reiterate the lessons they learnt about their own lives from the collective discussions during rehearsals. Having reached the stage of self-awareness, they seemingly 'lived' their lives on stage before audiences in ways that brought out the 'emotional truths' in their lives as Njūgūna, Njaramba (1993), Gīthiga (1995), and Coru (1995) attested. Equally significant, many of the audience were able to identify with the 'lived' reality on stage. Indeed, Njūgūna Muchendū, one of the major actors in *Maitū Njugīra* joined the cast because of his learning experience as a spectator in the *Ngaahika Ndeenda* performance in 1977 (Njūgūna, 13 August 1993). This kind of spectator learning was built into the opening songs of both productions. *Ngaahika Ndeenda* opened with a song (Mwīkū Mwīkū – where are you) that invited the audiences to open their ears and hearts and bridge the actor/spectator gulf. So did *Maitū Njugīra*, with its rousing opening song that asked those who were still apathetic and apolitical to 'wake up from their slumber'. The songs deliberately structured the performance as a discussion – *ūkai twaranirie*, meaning come let us reason together. By modelling prohibited social interactions in the contained space of performance, the actors were able to collectively encourage dialogue on questions that Ngūgī posed in his own novels which were, problematically, read mainly by the middle class. As such, reformulating Dwyer's question is appropriate. Even as it sensitized audiences to their material positions and problematized their point of observation, how was Kamīrīīthū modelling the social problems and their solutions as expressed by his fiction?

Kamīrīīthū emphasized the lessons to be learnt from the rehearsals, and the discussions that took place during those rehearsals and process were more important than final product. By demystifying the process of theatrical codification through open rehearsals, the Kamīrīīthū group exposed the constructedness of the performed text. By insisting on changes to the ending of *Maitū Njugīra*, the group also recognized how, in the contained world of performance, certain oppressive social relations that exist in the real world could be performed differently, with different outcomes. Through showing audiences their imbrication in oppressive social relations, the Kamīrīīthū plays sought to show them that a radically transformed world was a distinct possibility, and two participants compared their acting to a preacher speaking to a receptive congregation that could be moved to recognize where they fall short (Njūgūna and Njaramba, 13 August 1993).

The trouble is that the realization of that possibility depended on social processes that were then not on the horizon. While the Kamīrīīthū plays facilitated a whole new set of social relations among the diverse participants in the project who were confronted with their material positions, the conditions for transformative change were not ripe. Paradoxically, the participants' hyper-consciousness of class relations and their adoption of fairly Marxist language in my interviews with them sounded contrived, given the fact that at the time some of them were involved in some hierarchical relations with the rest of the cast members in the revived Kamīrīīthū productions, and that some of those who did not participate in these revivals were themselves in positions of authority in the civil service. This raises questions as to whether the participants had been fully committed to the kind of dialogue for which Kamīrīīthū has been celebrated. It also raises questions as to whether they envisaged structural transformation of the society that would protect their own sectional – particularly class and gender – interests. Ngũgĩ's participation in the theatre project allowed him access to the vitality of peasant creativity and to valuable lessons in the transcription and notation of traditional songs. For example, in numerous interviews, the only textual interventions that were attributed to the village participants were in the transcription, structuring and choreography of traditional songs. However, without Ngũgĩ's continued input, and given the state repression that followed the banning of theatre activities in the area in 1982 – they were deemed anti-development by the central government – none of the village participants were able to produce scripts or dances that could be said to directly reflect their growing confidence in the performing arts. However, Kamīrīīthū village reaped four rewards from the theatre effort. There was the transient glory of challenging the ruling elites of the late 1970s and early 1980s. The participants also proved that local languages were adequate vehicles for a major theatrical production, and that theatrical production need not happen in the hallowed performance spaces of the state capital and the major towns. But when the government banned the Kamīrīīthū group in March 1982 and burnt down their theatre, the greatest beneficiaries of the banning of the community-based theatre efforts and the building of the new polytechnic that replaced the community-built theatre were the landless squatters who had built their houses on part of the community centre's land. They were given free land by the government in Ndeiya, about six miles away, in order to make way peacefully for the construction of the polytechnic. Ironically, the people thank Ngũgĩ for the free land. To this day, the local people call the former cultural centre, 'Ha Ngũgĩ', meaning, 'Ngũgĩ's place/space'.

As I argue in *Ngũgĩ wa Thiong'o's Drama* (2007: 200), there are actually three phases of Kamīrīīthū that might correspond to what Harry Elam identifies as efficacious, effective and entertaining theatrical performances. In his seminal study of the 1960s black social protest theatre, *Taking it to the Streets: The Social Protest Theater of Luis Valdez and Amiri Baraka* (2007), Elam valorizes efficacious performances which move audiences to act as participants. These Elam compares to congregations in ritual performances. Audiences undertake self-searching and delve into the social meaning of the performances. According to Elam, these performances are different from those that are merely entertaining and which allow the audiences to remain spectators removed from the ritual action. He affirms the fact that participation testifies to the meaning of the play's action for the participant community, positing the audience in the subject position (127). Yet, Elam warns also that social context is integral to the efficacy of the social protest performances. These work not in a vacuum, '... but in synergistic communion with the urgent social activities occurring in society' (24). Using Elam's argument, I identify three phases/faces of Kamīrīīthū in Kenya: the effective *Ngaahika Ndeenda* performances of 1977; the efficacious

Kamīrīīthū in Retrospect 57

Maitū Njugīra Kamīrīīthū of 1982, and the commercial entertainment Kamīrīīthū of 1995/96. At least two of these Kamīrīīthūs (1977 and 1995/96), lack what Elam calls 'urgency' – the social processes that would have made performances efficacious, rather than merely effective or entertaining. In his analysis of the 1977 Kamīrīīthū, Frank Youngman argued that however radical that performance sounded, it still needed to be connected to organized economic and political struggle to be effectively counter-hegemonic (1986: 232). Such struggles were not on the horizon at the time of the first Kamīrīīthū performances. Neither the sense of disenfranchisement and the frustrations with the Kenyan social and political climate, nor the political oppression had yet reached crisis proportions. To paraphrase Elam, there was no 'urgency' – the social inequalities that *Ngaahika Ndeenda* so adequately mirrors were not by themselves adequate as a catalyst for the kind of structural crisis that would lead to the dismantling of the dominant power structure. However, by 1982, Kenya was rapidly deteriorating into the kind of police state dramatized in *Maitū Njugīra*. The objective conditions were ripe for the social strife and the triumph of the dispossessed that the play predicted. And because of its efficaciousness, the performance of the play attracted severe reprisals leading to the banning of the theatre group, the destruction of their theatre, and the exile of its main proponents in the most repressive period in independent Kenyan history. Clearly, in the eyes of the repressive state, Ngũgĩ was Kamīrīīthū and Kamīrīīthū was Ngũgĩ. But the banning of the performances only drove the 'performance texts' into underground reading circles where the title song of the production became a rallying cry for those who were no longer willing to endure their subjugation and urgently called for immediate reform of the oppressive structure. It is ironic that when conditions were riper for Kenyan theatre generally to play a more instrumental role in the political and social changes taking place in Kenya in the early 1990s, the revival of Kamīrīīthū was conceived as cultural and commercial entertainment. Although the social conditions were 'urgent', the Kamīrīīthū group did not link their theatrical production with the urgent and political activities occurring in Kenya. The choice of beer halls as performance spaces and the informing ideas behind the performances effectively altered the environmental conditions that would have lent efficacy to the Kamīrīīthū revivals. A humorous caricature of the original Kamīrīīthū was brought out by some of the penitent members of the original Kamīrīīthū production to welcome Ngũgĩ back to his home village when he ended his 22-year exile in August 2004. As a sanitized version of the *Ngaahika Ndeenda* that survived the commercial performances, this particular performance was supposed to mark a new beginning for Kamīrīīthū, and there was talk of reviving theatre activity in the village now that its great son had returned home. It remains to be seen ten years later whether a Kamīrīīthū resurgence at Kamīrīīthū itself will be forthcoming.

It is possible to come down too hard on the participants in the third phase of Kamīrīīthū for bastardizing one of the key texts of theatrical resistance. But interviews with the participants in that group (14 out of the original 35 core participants) point to some of the major paradoxes of Kamīrīīthū. Not all participants joined the original effort because they believed in its informing logic. Some wanted to be part of the latest fad in the village; some wanted to be closer to Ngũgĩ, one of the most accomplished sons of the village. Some hoped to refine their talents in the hope of eventually finding well-paid work as performance artists. It is also an understated fact that a significant portion of the participants joined the theatre effort in the hope of deriving some material rewards. With the plays banned before they could financially benefit, they waited for an opportune moment to get what some called their 'fair share' of the profits from the play.

A retrospective look at Kamīrīīthū reveals some interesting paradoxes. The literacy and theatre projects attempted to circumvent and interrogate the failures of the government of the day. Because the participants did not involve the state machinery in their functions, the patrimonial central government became wary of independent development efforts that it did not control. The group was therefore subjected to state surveillance, Ngũgĩ was eventually detained for a year in 1977 for 'anti-government propaganda', theatre activities were banned in the area for hampering 'development' and the community theatre razed by the government in 1982. Ngũgĩ and the intellectual cadre around him were hounded into exile in the same year, leading to the virtual death of radical theatre efforts in the area. Without the intellectual elite to craft politically conscious theatre when the political situation really called for it in the early 1990s, the Kamīrīīthū participants commercialized their radical performances from the 1970s and early 1980s. It would appear from the foregoing that Kamīrīīthū needed Ngũgĩ in order to survive. This is problematic because arguably a really participatory theatre effort should have been able to outlive the contributions of a core group.

BIBLIOGRAPHY

Brown, Nicholas (1999) 'Revolution and Recidivism: The Problem of Kenyan History in the Plays of Ngũgĩ wa Thiong'o', *Research in African Literatures*. 30 (4): 57-73.
Desai, Gaurav (1990) 'Theatre as Praxis: Discursive Strategies in African Popular Theatre', *African Studies Review*. 33 (1): 65-91.
Dwyer, Paul (2004) 'Making Bodies Talk in Forum Theatre', *Research in Drama Education*. 9 (2): 199-210.
Elam, Harry J. Jr. (1997) *Taking it to the Streets: The Social Protest Theater of Luis Valdez and Amiri Baraka*, Ann Arbor: University of Michigan Press.
Kerr, David (1995) *African Popular Theatre*, London: James Currey.
Kidd, Ross (1983) 'Popular Theatre and Popular Struggle in Kenya: The Story of Kamiriithu', *Race and Class*, XXIV (3): 287-304.
Ndĩgĩrĩgĩ, Gĩchingiri (1999) 'Kenyan Theatre after Kamīrīīthū', *The Drama Review*. 43: (2) 72-93.
— (2007) *Ngũgĩ wa Thiong'o's Drama and the Kamīrīīthū Popular Theatre Experiment*, Trenton NJ: Africa World Press.
Ngũgĩ wa Thiong'o (1980) *Ngaahika Ndeenda* (with Ngũgĩ wa Mĩriĩ). Nairobi: Heinemann.
— *Maitũ Njugĩra*. Unpublished manuscript.
Youngman, Frank (1986) *Adult Education and Socialist Pedagogy*, London: Croom Helm.

INTERVIEWS CITED

Mūirūrī, Coru. 15 March 1995.
Mūturi wa Nyambura. 20 March 1995.
Mwaūra, Gīthiga. 20 February 1995, 14 March 1995.
Njaramba Kaguora. 13 August 1993, 21 February 1995, 14 March 1995.
Njūgūna Mūchendū. 13 August 1993.

Wole Soyinka & Ngũgĩ wa Thiong'o
Plays in production

JAMES GIBBS & MUGO MUHIA

Two giants of African theatre, Wole Soyinka and Ngũgĩ wa Thiong'o, have been involved in very different kinds of work, and the differences are apparent in the production histories of their work that follows. To keep the Soyinka part of this chapter within manageable proportions, only one of his plays is considered here. It is, appropriately, a well-known work, and one that has been given both relatively modest and extensively reviewed 'main stage' productions: *Death and the King's Horseman* (1976). The Ngũgĩ part of this chapter, prepared with limited resources and under pressure of time, seeks to suggest the scope of his theatre work over the whole of his career. It draws attention to the analyses of the play-making processes that he has been involved with and makes very direct links with several of the articles in this volume.

Death and the King's Horseman, 1976. A play in production: an extract from a longer playography by James Gibbs

Written in Cambridge when Soyinka was in residence at Churchill College (September 1973), *Horseman* was given a 'read through' there. It has become Soyinka's most widely studied play, but probably not his most widely performed. (That title must, I think, go to *The Trials of Brother Jero*, 1964). The Cambridge matrix was significant for the play's genesis, and in *Myth, Literature and the African World* Soyinka has written about the 'colonial' attitudes he encountered that resulted in him delivering his lectures in the Anthropology Department! (The study of mankind may be man, but the study of Africans is anthropology.) Soyinka has also spoken of the influence on him of the bust of Churchill in the college where he was accommodated. I take that reference – see 'Who's Afraid of Elesin Oba?' and *Orisha Liberates the Mind*, (1992: 15-16) – to suggest that the bust prompted consideration of issues of leadership and determination.

Although Cambridge and Churchill may have 'triggered' the play, the story or 'plot' is also important. Soyinka had been aware of the episode around which the play revolves – the interrupted ritual suicide in Oyo – for more than a decade. It had, for example, been brought to his attention by Ulli Beier in 1960, when Beier put it forward as providing a resonant episode for a play to mark Nigeria's independence. It seems Soyinka mulled over the account he had been given and that the play, when it came, flowed freely onto the page. Perhaps surprisingly, he does not seem to have had qualms about handling such a recent event (1946), and does not seem to have considered the position of those in Oyo who were 'involved' in one way or another in the events he put on stage. I see no evidence that he undertook any research into particular rituals or sought out the political details involved in the events he was, in a sense, dramatizing. Rather than explore a particular historical instance, Soyinka sought to convey what he perceived as a general truth using a generic 'Yoruba setting'.

In this context, it is significant to note that he placed near the dramatic centre of the play the moment when Elesin Oba embarks on a 'Dance to Death'. A transcribed conversation between Soyinka and Beier about the play confirms that the playwright believes that special people holding particular positions in Yoruba society are able to die by an act of will. The audience is asked to accept this possibility. Ngũgĩ wa Thiong'o, on the other side of the continent and grappling with a history in which settler responsibility for a death was excused in part because of the belief that Africans were able to will themselves to death, rejected it. Ngũgĩ is at his most forthright in *Detained: A Writer's Prison Diary* (1981) where he responds to Karen Blixen's account of the death of Kitosch. A victim of settler brutality, Kitosch is not considered a murder victim because, injured, bound and locked up overnight, he willed himself to die. Ngũgĩ's comment on Blixen's account includes the following: 'Medical science was even brought in to support the wish-to-die theory. This was supposed to be a psychological peculiarity of the African. He wants to die and he dies' (1981: 36). Against this kind of background, and having to fight these sorts of myths, Ngũgĩ's response to Elesin's 'wish-to-die' is understandable. For Soyinka and Beier on sources of *Horseman*, see *Orisha Liberates the Mind* (1992: 14-15); on 'wish to die', *Death and the King's Horseman: A Conversation between Wole Soyinka and Ulli Beier* (1993).

Death and the King's Horseman was published in 1975 and given its premiere in 1976 when it was the Convocation Play for the University of Ile-Ife – later Obafemi Awolowo University (OAU). The production inaugurated the vast Oduduwa Theatre, a new space for Soyinka to direct in. In the course of a favourable review, Gerald Moore (1977) referred to problems caused by the 'vast volume of air separating the players from each other and from' the audience. While Moore was receptive to the play, others had profound reservations, and we should remember that the Ibadan–Ife Group of Radical Critics who were linked with *Positive Review* enjoyed considerable influence at this period. There were those who saw the play as part of a preoccupation, apparent in the work of Ola Rotimi, with 'beaded crowns'. This allegation was short-hand for a reactionary interest with the panoply of feudalism. (Biodun Jeyifo: 'Soyinka Demythologised', (unpub. c. 1983) and (1985) 'Ideology and Tragedy', in *The*

Truthful Lie: Essays in a Sociology of African Drama; and Niyi Osundare (1988), 'Theatre of the Beaded Curtain: Nigerian Drama and the Kabiyesi Syndrome, *Okike* (Enugu), 27/28: 99-113). Soyinka felt the ideological pressure exerted by these colleagues sufficiently oppressive to respond to it in 'Who's Afraid of Elesin Oba?'

Soyinka begins his 'Author's Note' to *Horseman* by referring to the 'factual account' of the 'intertwining' of 'the lives of Elesin (Olori Elesin), his son and the Colonial District Officer' that, he asserts 'still exists in the archives of the British Colonial Administration' and that had 'disastrous results'. (I found no account of the episode in the National Archives at Ibadan, but Pierre Verger entered into correspondence with Robert Barry Kerr who wrote to him (on 14 June 1957). Kerr stated that he 'was District Officer Oyo during the installation of the Alafin of Oyo in 1946' and that he 'pulled the Olokunesin (Master of Horse) from a procession in which he was performing a dance of death preparatory to committing suicide in order not to survive his master, the late Alafin.' Soyinka moves on to observe that it is 'the bane of themes of this genre ... that they are no sooner employed creatively than they acquire the facile tag of "clash of cultures"'. This he described as 'a prejudicial label which, quite apart from its frequent misapplication, presupposes a potential equality *in every given situation* of the alien culture and the indigenous on the actual soil of the latter.' (WS's emphasis.) He urged the interpreter of his play 'to direct his vision instead to the far more difficult and risky task of eliciting the play's threnodic essence'. This essence is hard to define, and harder still to convey. Indeed it is helpful to leave the Note aside and listen to Soyinka in a different vein. In a 1992 interview, he is quoted as saying:

> If you look at the play very carefully, I think, you'll find it really turns out to be an affirmation of life, of the principle of sacrifice, the principle of the scapegoat. The significance is, in fact, the assurance of continuity. It is not so much about death. I think it's more the preoccupation with the mysteries of transition, really trying to explore this normally intangible space through which we presumably pass coming into this world and through which we presumably must pass to join the ancestors. (Soyinka to Portnoy, 1992: 2)

Since 1976 when Soyinka directed the premiere, the play has been produced in, at least, Ghana, the US, the UK, and the RSA. There have been a number of Nigerian productions, some quite distinctive. Issues raised by the productions have included the presentation of the white characters/caricatures and the 'problem' of communicating Yoruba values. The second point provided material for Kacke Gotrik's (1990) study of various productions of the play, while, back in Western Nigeria, the situation has been considered from a different point of view and questions have been raised about the language(s) of the play. These include the discussion about whether parts or all of it should be performed in Yoruba. An admired Yoruba translation has been prepared by Akinwumi Isola, but, controversially, he has translated even the lines spoken by Simon Pilkings, Jane and Joseph.

Horseman has been given a number of high profile productions, three by Soyinka who has also seen a number of others. Among the important productions are those presented by Manchester Royal Exchange Theatre, PACT (South Africa) and the National Theatre (London). Again and again, the script has unleashed powerful creative forces that have had an astounding impact on audiences. In so far as the theatre can change society, I would submit that the productions in Chicago, New York, Manchester, London and South Africa have provided opportunities for theatre audiences to reflect. White audiences have had a chance to glimpse the way others see them, and those with an African heritage have been told a story about 'how the rain began to beat them'.

The US productions directed by Soyinka have been particularly important for shedding light on how creative and critical people interact, and on Soyinka as a director. His 1988 New York production prompted a review by Frank Rich of the *New York Times* – the notorious 'Butcher of Broadway'. Rich's remarks and the influence he wielded spurred Soyinka into print in a way that made the exchange part of a wider encounter, a running battle or 'continuing exchange'. The conflict surfaced again in relation to Soyinka's production of *A Play of Giants* (see below) after Rich asked: 'Is Soyinka a good director?' This is a question that Nigerian critics have generally avoided out of respect for Soyinka, and that UK-based critics have had no opportunity to consider – because Soyinka hasn't directed anything in the UK since 1959. Soyinka spoke to Portnoy about what he regards as 'dishonest criticism' and added: 'One such was the case of Monsieur Rich; this tyrant sits on the pages of *The New York Times*.' Soyinka went on to characterize Rich's case as one of 'megalomania, sheer megalomania' (1992: 7-8).

Inevitably, directors of Soyinka's work have been curious to know what the playwright thinks of their handling of his work. He has honoured invitations to attend performances and has taken part in Q and A sessions after 'the curtain has come down'. Those trying to draw him out on the major London production (2009) seem to have found him tight-lipped. However, the Lime Interview posted on the Collective Artistes site included the following quote:

> I thought it was a marvellous spectacle. I had irritating moments – I always do. When actors are lazy about new words, especially names – when they don't give names their correct value. Give them a Russian name and they pronounce it properly... Yes, I find that very irritating.

Premiere:
December 1976, Oduduwa University Theatre of Ife, December 1977, Dir. Soyinka, with Jimi Solanke (Elesin). See Moore (1977 and 1978).

Other productions include:
1979 October-December, Goodman Theatre, Chicago, transferred to J. F. Kennedy Centre for the Performing Arts, Washington DC (December), dir. Soyinka, with Norman Matlock (Elesin); Ben Halley Jr (Praise-singer); Celestine Heard (Iyaloja); Terry Alexander (Olunde). See Soyinka interviewed by Chuck Mike and by Sophia Jackson, *This is Lime* (http://www.thisislime.net/interviews/theatre). From the former comes the anecdote about the 'leading

lady who had to be sacked', p. 10. From the latter comes the following: 'When I directed *Death and the King's Horseman* in Chicago that was something I enjoyed doing. I was working with actors who had never worked on that kind of material in their lives and it really was like creating something completely new. They were professionals who had worked on traditional American theatre but this was a new world which I had to induct them (into) so that particular production I have fond memories of.'

Norman Matlock wrote on his experiences of auditioning for the play and of playing Elesin (1980). He referred to the audience reaction: '... the Africans [were] enjoying the hell out of it, while the Americans [were] simply enjoying.'

1984 University of Ibadan Arts Theatre, dir. Segun Ojewuyi.

1986 February, Teatro Accademico dell'Università dell'Aquila, as *La Morte e il Cavaliere del Re* at the XII Festival Internazionale del Teatro Universitario, L'Aquila, dir. Giancarlo Gentilucci. Also performed at Liège (Belgium).

1987 March, Vivian Beaumont Theatre, Lincoln Center, New York City, dir. Soyinka at the invitation of Greg Mosher, with Ben Halley Jr. Olohun-iyo); Earle Hyman (Elesin); Trazana Beverley (Iyaloja); Celestine Heard (Ekeji-Oja); Sylvia Best (the Bride); Eriq La Salle (Olunde); Alan Coates (Simon Pilkings); Jill Larson (Jane Pilkings); Ernest Perry Jr. (Sergeant Amusa); Abdoulaye N'gom (Joseph); Dillon Evans (The Resident); Graeme Malcolm (Aide de Camp); Roderick McLachlan (H.R.H. The Prince); Erika Petersen (His Consort); Robert Cenedella (Conductor).

The critical response was extensive and, as indicated above, Soyinka reacted to the views of Frank Rich in an exchange that then took on a life of its own:

- Dennis, Martine. 'Soyinka Fights On', *The African Guardian* (Lagos), 16 April 1987, 23. (Subtitled: 'The Laureate reacts to adverse reviews of his play'; this account includes quotes from Rich and Soyinka on reactions to the New York production of *Horseman*, and includes some general comments on relations between Soyinka and the New York press.)
- Hill, Holly. 'Vicious Circle', *The Times* (London), 6 April 1987, 17.
- Morrison, Toni. 'More thoughts on *Death and the King's Horseman*,' *The New Theatre Review*, 1: 2 (Summer 1987), 11.
- Reed, Ishmael. 'Soyinka among the Monoculturalists', *Black American Literature Forum* (Terre Haute), 22, 4 (Winter 1988), 705-9. (Also in *New Theatre Review* 1: 2 (1987), 8-9; and *Writin' is Fightin': Thirty-Seven Years of Boxing on Paper*, New York: Athenaeum, (1988), 109-17. (An important reflection on experiences of plays in performance.)
- Rich, Frank. 'Review of *Death and the King's Horseman* Lincoln Theater', *New York Times*, 2 March, 1987. (The attitudes underlying this review were discussed at length in Soyinka's session with H. L. Gates Jr, see *The New Theatre Review*, 1: 2, and *The Southern Review* (Baton Rouge), Summer 1987.)
- The discussion continued, revived by the inclusion of 'Poet-Mortem for a "Death..."' in *Art, Dialogue and Outrage* (1998: 330-344) and then by the reviews of that book. See, for example, Jonathan Coe, 'Wole's Leftovers', *The Guardian* (London), 5 August 1988, and David Caute, *TLS*, 13-29,

September 1988, p. 1042. For Nigerian comment, see Chinweizu. 'The Chinweizu Observatory: Critics Rights: Admonitions to Soyinka', *Vanguard*, 6 November, 1988, 7.

1983 University of Nsukka, with Esiaba Irobi (Elesin Oba). Note Irobi subsequently played the role 'several times' between 1985 and 1989. See Esiaba Irobi, 'Legacy: Theory and Practice of Postcolonial Performance' http://muse.jhu.edu/journals/research_in_african_literatures/summary/v042/42.4.diala.html.

1988 Lagos National Theatre production, dir. Osayin. See Mofe Damijo, Richard. 'Beyond Soyinka's *Death and the King's Horseman*.' *National Concord* (Lagos), 18 May, 7.

1988 Nsukka production, dir. Eni Jones Umuko. See Oguibe, Olu. 'A ritual tremor', *West Africa* (London), 4 April 1988, 5989.

1990, February, Lagos Diamond Productions by Bayo Oduneye, with Femi Ogunjobi ('Eleshin'); Ajayi Olatide (Praise Singer/Olohuniyo); Femi Euba (Pilkings); Taiwo Ajai Lycett (Iyaloja); Dede Mabiaku (Olunde); Albert Odulate (Amusa); Nkechi Ezechi (Jane). Funded by Nigerian International Bank (NIB). See:

- Adeboye, Lanre and Dapo Adeniyi. '*Death* on Stage', *Daily Times* (Lagos), 3 February 1990. (Refers to Oduneye's production as the fifth in Nigeria since Soyinka directed it in 1976, and indicates that the performances began at 2 pm each day of the run from 7–11 February. Presumably this curtain-up time was a reaction to after-dark dangers and reflected the security problems that have hindered the development of theatre in Nigeria. The performance on the 6 February was a Command Performance. Oduneye quoted as saying 'One of our objectives will be to find contemporary relevance for this historical piece.')
- Ayoola, Tosin. 'Teaching Soyinka a few tricks', *West Africa* (London), 915 April 1990, 606. (Reports that Oduneye 'made a success of what is commonly regarded as the most difficult of Soyinka's plays.' Draws attention to the celebratory element in the production and 'an age old Yoruba tradition that when the king dies, his horseman must be sacrificed'.)
- Enaibe, Edmond. 'Before the toast to *Death*...' *The Republic*, 20 February 1990, 13. (Expresses concern over various aspects of the publicity and of the audience experience.)
- Ette, Mercy. 'Reliving History on Stage', *Newswatch* (Lagos), 19 February 1990, 20. (Praises the author, director, and several performers, especially Olatide; reported unfavourably on Euba.)
- Kargbo, Kolosa. 'The Horseman, the Stallion and the Riddle of Death', *Prime People* (Lagos), 23 February–1 March 1990. (Praises set, lighting, costumes and dirging. Regards 'dignity' as a key word in summarizing the action of the play. Considers Euba's Pilkins (sic) was a revelation. Describes the play as 'a modern day master's parable of excess'.)

1990, November–December, Manchester Royal Exchange Theatre Company, dir. Phyllida Lloyd, with George Harris (Elesin Oba); Claire Benedict (Iyaloja);

Simon Dormandy (Pilkings); Peter Adegboyego Badejo (Praise Singer and choreography); Muraina Oyelami (musical director and composer); Anthony Ward (design). The production was 'in the round' in what had been a commercial building – the Royal Exchange, and the direction was strongly collaborative. Badejo, a veteran of many Soyinka productions, was a crucial contributor. The production was hailed as the UK premiere but it followed a Hull production in July 1983 by Chris Kamlongera (see Walton 1991 for a reference to this). The Manchester production was very extensively reviewed, but I shall only direct attention to three reviews and one academic article:

- Bandele Thomas, Biyi. 'The British Premiere of a 20th Century Classic', *Home News* (Lagos), 29 Nov–4 Dec 1990, 13. (Favourable review that compares Lloyd's production with those by Osanyin and Oduneye. Comments on Iyaloja's 'quaint' pronunciation of Yoruba. Considers that Badejo's decision to translate lines into Yoruba during the trance scene worked well.)
- Barber, Karin. 'Drums and Shame', *Times Higher Educational Supplement* (London), 14 12 90.
- Hunt, Albert. 'A masterpiece in black and white', *The Guardian* (London), 24 November. 1990. (Regards Soyinka as scathing about the whites and inviting 'African audiences to question themselves too.' Describes 'the dirge at the end' as making 'one of the most powerful moments I have ever experienced in the theatre.' Says the play 'puts exciting political theatre back on the agenda.')
- Rohmer, Martin. 'Wole Soyinka's 'Death and the King's Horseman', Royal Exchange Theatre, Manchester, *New Theatre Quarterly*, 1994 (February, 10: (37) 57-69: http://dx.doi.org/10.1017/S0266464X00000099, Published online: 15 January 2009. (A well-illustrated, closely argued and substantial account.)

1994 *Iku Olokun Esin*, National Arts Theatre, Lagos, dir. Ojewuyi.
1995 September, BBC 3, dir. Alby James.
2000 Syracuse Stage, dramaturg/ creative advisor Ojewuyi.
2001 Western Zone of the National Association of Nigerian Theatre Practitioners (NANTAP) as part of the Festival of Nigerian Plays (FESTINA 2001) at the Glover Memorial Hall, Lagos.
2004 at the MUSON Centre, Lagos, dir. Ahmed Yerima, with Olu Jacobs (Elesin); Kunle Bamtefa (Olohun Iyo); Olawuni (Iyalode); St. Pius Amolo (Pilkings); Iyabo Amoke (Jane Pilkings); Wale Ojo (Olunde); Tunji Sotimirin (Sgt. Amusa); Toyin Osinaike (Joseph). See Ayorinde, Steve. 'Artistes Celebrate Soyinka with play', *Punch* 8 July 2004, http://www.cafeafricana.com/tributes-wole-soyinka.html. Describes 'Tuesday's command performance, at which an abridged version was performed. Soyinka, it seems, left early. Yerima was quoted as saying: 'We have played down the mastery of Soyinka's poetic language and extended the ethos to include the dances of Soyinka's music, Soyinka's ritual drama and, most importantly, the sensibilities of Soyinka's people in the form of instrumentation, metaphors, symbols, proverbs and the Yoruba language. The idea is to carry over the communal spirit and chorus through intentions and

sometimes, through the extension of the ritual material which belong to us in the first place.' (Note the production celebrated Soyinka's 70th birthday. It, and a production of the play in Yoruba, was taken to Abeokuta.) Ayorinde wrote: when Soyinka 'left the presentation, midway, nobody could tell why.'

2004 Philadelphia Theatre Company at the Lantern Theatre, with Forrest McClendon (Elesin).

2004 February, Washington State University, Pullman, WA, dir. Euba. Soyinka watched a performance that was followed by a panel discussion.

2004 April, performed at the Jos Festival of Theatre, Plateau State, Nigeria. See Oteh, 2012. (Note: In the six Jos Festivals held between 2004 and 2012, four Soyinka titles were presented: *Horseman* (2004), *Lion and Jewel* (2006), *Madmen and Specialists* (2008) *and Brother Jero* (2009). This represents a substantial commitment to a national dramatist.)

2006 in the Taylor Theatre, University of North Carolina, Greensboro, dir. Alan Cook, with Randy McMullen (design) and Robin Gee (choreography).

2007 September, the Fehinty African Theater Ensemble (FATE) at Bailiwick Arts Center, Chicago, dir. Adekunle Akingboju, 'a Nigerian-born engineering student at the University of Illinois at Chicago'.

2007 November, Jos Repertory Theatre presented the play at South Dallas Cultural Center. See http://www.pegasusnews.com/news/2007/nov/08/teatro-dallas-south-dallas-cultural-center-announc/

2008 February, staged by St. Edward's Theater Department, Austin, Texas, dir. Stephen Gerald. (Soyinka attended both a rehearsal of this 'theatre in the round production' and a Gala Performance that was followed by a Q and A Session.)

2008 February, the St. Louis Black Repertory Theater and the SIUC Theater Department, dir. Ojewuyi. (Soyinka once again present.)

2008 May, *Mort et le Cavalier du Roi* in Dakar http://newsletterappa.over-blog.com/article-19511833-6.html. Actors from Senegal, France and Congo were involved.

2008 November, at Kalamazoo College's Festival Playhouse, with Folabo-Ajayi Soyinka (choreography) and Femi Euba involved in directing. Soyinka took part in a Q and A.

2008 December at Terra Kultura, Lagos, two Sunday performances, dir. Wole Oguntokun. Supported by GT Bank. (See as part of the annual Soyinka Season.)

2009 February – July, as part of the Oregon Shakespeare Festival in the Angus Bowmer Theatre, dir. Chuck Smith, with Ojewuyi (dramaturge). See Oregon Shakespeare Festival·587 videos http://seattlepi.nwsource.com/local/386116_shakespeare03.html accessed 2008 11 04. Observes that *Horseman* is 'rarely produced'.

Iku Olokun Esin (Yoruba translation by Akinwumi Isola), presented at the National Theater, Lagos, dir. Olusegun Ojewuyi. (Part of the story of the Nigerian National Theatre building, that was constructed for Festac '77 by a Bulgarian company to a Bulgarian design, is told by Yerima in *African Theatre:*

Companies. Soyinka spoke of a Bulgarian theatre building he admired to Mike 1986: 4.)

2009 April, Royal National Theatre, London; dir. Rufus Norris with Javier de Frutos (choreographer); Katrina Lindsay (design); Lucian Msamati (Elesin); Oguntokun (liaison London – Lagos). See *Sunday Times* 5 stars, *Independent* and *Guardian* so so; *Mail* – why always blame the whiteman? See Gibbs and Olatokun in *NEXT*; Sierz in *Tribune*; Awoyokun on nigeriavillagesquare. Soyinka's comments in Lime interviews quoted above.

WORKS CITED

Gotrick, Kacke (1990) 'Soyinka and *Death and the King's Horseman* or, How Does Our Knowledge – or Lack of Knowledge – of Yoruba Culture Affect Our Interpretation?' In Raoul Granqvist (ed.) *Signs and Signals: Popular Culture in Africa*, Umea Studies in the Humanities 99, Umea: Almqvist and Wiskell International, 137-48.

Moore, Gerald (1977) 'Soyinka's New Play', Review of *Death and the King's Horseman*, *West Africa*, 10 January, 60-61.

—— (1978; Second Edition) *Wole Soyinka*, London: Evans.

Walton, J. Michael (1991) 'Second Death', *Times Higher Education Supplement* (London), 21 December.

Ngũgĩ's plays in production: Mũgo Mũhĩa with James Gibbs

Gĩkũyũ nĩ ooigire:
(Aine ta arĩ mũgoiyo)
Thegere igĩrĩ itiremagwo nĩ mwatũ,
Ũugi wa mũũndũ ũmwe ndũrĩmaga,
Rwambo rũmwe rũtiambaga ndaarwa,
Rũtuungu rũmwe rũtiraaragia mwaki,
Kĩara kĩmwe gĩtiũragaga ndaa,
Kamũingĩ kooyaga ndĩrĩ. (116-17)

Gĩkũyũ once said:
(sings)
Two porcupines can lift a beehive
One man's skill does not till the land
One peg cannot spread a hide
One log cannot last a fire
One finger cannot kill a louse
Many people make work lighter.

Introduction

The Gĩkũyũ proverbs quoted above are used by Gĩcaamba in *I Will Marry When I Want* to draw attention to the mutual support and the team effort essential in the production of a play. For Ngũgĩ wa Thiong'o (hereafter 'Ngũgĩ') collaboration in the theatre is continuous from the suggestion of an idea for a play through the process of rehearsal to performance. The proverbs also draw attention to the theme of African communalism that runs through Ngũgĩ's work. In *Decolonising the Mind* (1986), he revealingly describes drama as an effort involving many hands, and as 'an activity among other activities, often drawing its energy from those other activities' (37). In that book he gives specific examples of the contributions made by those involved with him in community theatre in the creative process. He writes, for example, that the members of the company were concerned that the various characters, depending on age and occupation, be given appropriate language: 'An old man cannot speak like that' they would say. 'If you want him to have dignity, he has to use this or that kind of proverb.' Levels of language-use and the nuances of words and phrases were discussed heatedly.

Ngũgĩ makes it clear that political, economic and ideological issues were also debated!

From the production histories below it can be seen that Ngũgĩ moved from writing for drama competitions in educational institutions to involvement with generating politically relevant productions for a specific community. The scripts of those productions, on which he might be said to have acted sometimes as a writer, sometimes as a facilitator – or editor, or, to use his own term, 'a messenger', have since been taken from their original contexts, translated and performed in very different circumstances. When work prepared in Gĩkũyũ for performance in the Kamĩrĩĩthũ Community Education and Cultural Centre (hereafter 'Kamĩrĩĩthũ') is translated into Kiswahili and put on in Nairobi, or translated into English and put on in London, those involved encounter a variety of opportunities and challenges.

The stream of major works by Ngũgĩ, the forty-three interviews with him collected in a (2006) volume edited by Sander and Lindfors, and newer material accessible on-line provide fascinating first-hand accounts of productions and nuanced descriptions of political encounters. That revealing material is complemented by the accounts of students of Ngũgĩ's work and by assessments prepared by some of those involved with Theatre for Development in Africa. The reviews of the productions, the testimonies of those involved, and the critical scrutiny of theatre historians, some listed below, also give indications of how transitions have been handled. However, the state of data collection regarding African drama means that only a sketch has emerged, and the list that follows is offered as 'a work in progress'.

Production history

***The Rebels*, 1961** (published in *Penpoint* (Makerere), 11, Oct 1961, 59-69); and in *This Time Tomorrow*, East African Literature Bureau, (see below).

1961, produced by Makerere University students, as part of an Inter-Hall drama competition.

1962, April, broadcast on Radio Uganda. See: Gĩchingiri wa Ndĩgĩrĩgĩ (2007), *Ngũgĩ wa Thiongo's Drama and the Kamĩrĩĩthũ Popular Theatre Experiment*, Trenton NJ: Africa World Press, 13-14.

***The Wound in the Heart* 1962** (published in *Penpoint*, 13 (October 1962), 23-9, and later in the collection, *This Time Tomorrow*, 1967).

1962, Makerere University students for Inter-Hall drama competition. See Gĩchingiri wa Ndĩgĩrĩgĩ (2007:13).

***The Black Hermit,* 1962** (published AWS 51 (1963).

1962, November, Makerere College Students Dramatic Society at Uganda National Theatre, Kampala, as part of independence celebrations. See Karienye, Yohanna. 'African Viewpoint: *The Black Hermit*', *Kenya Weekly News*, 2 November 1962, 21. Also Carpenter, Peter. 'Theatre in East and West Africa', *Drama*, 69 (1963), 34. Ngũgĩ has spoken about the 'hazy' quality of this early work in interviews collected by Sander and Lindfors (2006: 144).

1964, Kitante Hill School, dir. John Morris and Rupert Barnes, with Godfrey Lutwana (Kĩariĩ) Angelo Nsubuga (Nyobi). See Aiyegbusi, T. 'Good... but Why Change Setting', *Sunday Nation*, 21 June 1964.

1966, July, Thompson Falls High School, Kenyan Premiere, dir. R. Barnes, and Winston Theuri, also put on in Nyahururu, 8-9 July 1966. See: Nation Reporter, 'The First Kenya Performance of James Ngũgĩ's Play *The Black Hermit*', *Daily Nation*, Nairobi, 5 July 1966, 5. (Note: I suspect many educational institutions, in many countries, must have put on this play, but limitations of time and research resources mean that this record has to 'stand in' for them.)

1970, February, The National Theatre Company at the Kenya Cultural Centre, dir. Seth Adagala. See: *Daily Nation*, '*The Black Hermit*', 27 February 1970; Mckinney, Liza, 'Two Plays – One Big Success', *Daily Nation*, Nairobi, 28 February 1970; Ngarĩ, Peter, 'The Challenge to Africans', *Daily Nation*, Nairobi, 24 February 1970; Also December, The National Theatre Company at the Kenya National Theatre, Nairobi, dir. Adagala. See: Oderrow, Mitch, 'Theatre revolution', *Daily Nation*, Nairobi, 12 April 1970. Note the use of The National Theatre, a 'contested space', and one that, Ngũgĩ complained, rarely hosted indigenous work.

1971, Shanzu Teachers' College, as part of Kenya National Drama Festivals, with Virgina Mugure (Nyobi). See Mckinney, Liza, 'Schools Drama Festivals', *Daily Nation*, Nairobi, 28 February 1970, 8.

1971, January, University of Lagos. See Adegbiji, Segun, 'A Fruitful Year for drama', *Daily Times* (Lagos), 13 January 1971. (This example shows the script being staged 'far from home'.)

***This Time Tomorrow,* 1967** (published in a collection of three plays, Nairobi: EALB, n.d., possibly 1970/1. Ngũgĩ, it seems, 'had nasty experiences in dealing with Kenya-based publishing houses'. See Sander and Lindfors, p. 131.)

1967, November, broadcast in the BBC's African Theatre, Ndīgīrīgī, p. 13, and Cordeaux, Shirley (1970), 'The BBC's African Service's Involvement in African Theatre, *Research in African Literatures* 1: 2, Autumn, 147-55.

1975, July, Starehe Boys' Centre, as part of inter-house drama competition. See: Beaumont, Robert, 'Starehe Boys Centre Inter-house Drama', *Daily Nation*, Nairobi, 13 July 1975. (This is an example of the selection of Ngũgĩ's short works for performance in drama competitions. Note: Drama competitions have played an important role in the development of African theatre.

***The Trial of Dedan Kimathi* 1975,** by Ngũgĩ and Mīcere Mūgo. *Mzalendo Kīmathi* (Kiswahili translation); *Magerio ma Kīmathi* (Gĩkũyũ translation). In the Preface, the authors recall their contacts as under-graduates and their experiences after graduation. They refer to their political philosophies and their awareness of the (neglected) 'heroic peasant armed struggle against the British forces of occupation' (v). In 1971, the authors dreamed of co-authoring a play about neglected hero Dedan Kīmathi and in 1974 they realized that dream. In the course of preparing their text, they read and consulted widely, and, while taking responsibility for 'the faults and the shortcomings' in the text, they describe the work as the 'result of a collective effort'. Published Nairobi: Heinemann, Kenya, 1976, and then in the African Writers Series (AWS) by Heinemann (1977).

1975 October, premiere, the Nairobi University Free Travelling Theatre at the Kenya National Theatre, and on tour (1976), dir. Adagala. See Karanja, Mũgambi, 'Dramatic Trek Takes Theatre to the People', *Daily Nation*, Nairobi, 10 September 1976: 25. For Ngũgĩ on 'Free Travelling University Theatre', see Sander and Lindfors (2006: 145).

1977 October, FESTAC '77 Drama Group, at Kenya National Theatre, and at Festac '77 (Lagos), dir. Adagala. See Ngũgĩ, 'Enactments of Power: The Politics of Performance Space', *Tulane Drama Review* (1988-), 41. 3; (1997): 11-30. Also, see Ngũgĩ, (1981) on the Kenyan National Theatre. Ironically the despatch of the play to represent the nation in Lagos did not stop the persecution of Ngũgĩ. For reflection on the Festac/ FESTAC episode, see Wumi Raji (2009), *Long Dreams in Short Chapters*, Berlin: Lit Verlag der Dr W Hopf, 41.

[1977] Ngũgĩ *Detained*. On detention see Sander and Lindfors, (2006: 92-3);

1980 Tamaduni Players, open-air performance at the Green Hills Hotel, Nyeri, Kiswahili translation with Karanja Njoroge (Kīmathi). See K.N.A., 'Hundreds Flock to witness Trial', *Daily Nation*, Nairobi, 30. 07. 1980, 5. (In 1980, Ngũgĩ spoke of watching a Swahili version of the play that was presented to packed houses, even in rural areas. He also described the emotional responses of some members of the audience.) See Sander and Lindfors (2006: 125).

1982 Zimbabwe Association of Community Theatre (ZACT), dir. Ngũgĩ wa Mīrii. Production in Shona. (An instance of the sharing of Kenyan experiences.)

1982, March, Kamīrīthū Theatre Group planned to perform the play at the Kenya National Theatre, Nairobi, and then take it with *Maitũ Njũgĩra* to Zimbabwe. However, permission to perform was denied. See Muthai, Wahome,

'Licence hitch angers Ngugi,' *Daily Nation*, 11 March 1982. Quoted Bjørkman (2004:102).

1982 Chemichemi Drama, *Mzalendo Kīmathi*, YMCA Shauri Moyo Hostel, Nairobi. See: Mūtahi, Wahome, 'Moses Brought to Life', *Sunday Nation* (Nairobi), 12 December 1982: 10.

1984, October, Wazalendo Players 84 (or '84), at the Africa Centre, London, dir. Ngũgĩ and Dan Baron Cohen. Open rehearsals, a feature of some community/participatory theatre, were held at a variety of venues in London and these prompted discussions. From the interview Ngũgĩ gave to Eyoh (*Ufahamu*, 1985) and from Cohen's account, see below, it is apparent that an 'international' performance of a piece of Kenyan theatre was inevitably challenging. See http://escholarship.org/uc/internationalasufahamungugi, and Cohen, Dan Baron, 'Resistance to Liberation: Decolonizing the Mindful Body', in *Performance Research: On Risk*, eds Roger Gough and C. Macdonald. (Summer 1996), On-line.

> *Dan Baron Cohen provided the following analysis of backstage disagreements that surfaced during rehearsals:*
> ... but though Wazalendo charismatically dramatized the decolonizing of the mind through African culture of participation and 'public rehearsal' in the community stage, backstage the cast was fractured (even traumatized) by tensions which – though eloquently explained in terms of colonization – could not be resolved. At the time, I believed that this hidden and repressed contradiction arose from the uneven politicization and motivation of those involved, from the bruising discovery of an inner circle of 'Kenyans-in-exile' within the company who felt that its much proclaimed collective decision-making had to be subordinated to the needs of political prisoners, and from a primary commitment to the advance of the Kenyan liberation movement.

1987, University of Nairobi Free Travelling Theatre at National Theatre and at Kenyatta University, with Oby Obiero Odhiambo (Kīmathi) and Kariũki Gakuo (Mathenge).

1990, December, University of Nairobi Free Travelling Theatre at National Theatre.

1995, August, Sarakasi Theatre, Shade Hotel, Ngong, in Gĩkũyũ translation – *Magerio ma Kīmathi*. See 'Down but Not Out!', *Daily Nation* (Nairobi), 18 August 1995, 22.

2014, February, Claire Trevor School of Arts and Drama, University of California, Irvine, at the Contemporary Arts Center, dir. Jaye Austin Fraser, with Oge Agalule (Kīmathi). See Iliff, Anna, '*The Trial of Dedan Kīmathi*' http://www.ocregister.com/sections/newsletter. (See Ketu Katrak in this volume.)

Soyinka & Ngũgĩ: Plays in Production 73

Ngaahika Ndeenda/I Will Marry When I Want, 1977
The play marked Ngũgĩ's engagement with a distinctive kind of participatory theatre that evolved partly through dialogue and debate. For an illuminating description of the process and Ngũgĩ's role see *Decolonising the Mind* (1986). Also see Sander and Lindfors, where he is reported to have said 'my job was reduced to that of a messenger' (2006: 159). The production led to Ngũgĩ's political persecution at the hands of security forces under Jomo Kenyatta and Arap Moi. Ngũgĩ's detention (16 November1977 to 12 December 1978) had a huge impact on his thinking and on the evolution of participatory theatre in Kenya.

1977, Kamĩrĩĩthũ Theatre group, dir. Kamau Gecau and cast. Open rehearsals attracted large audiences. Performances of the play were banned by the Kiambu District Commissioner on 10 November 1977. Note: for the production two actors were cast in some of the roles: Mbothu wa Waciira/Choru wa Mũirũrĩ (Ahab Kĩoi); Jane Nyokabi/Nyambura wa Ngũgĩ (Jezebel); Wainaina wa Gĩkonyo /Ng'ang'a wa Waciira (Ikuua wa Nditika); Ngigĩ wa Wachiira/Karanja wa Mwanĩki (Samuel Ndugĩre); Wakonyo wa Waiganjo / Gĩtĩri wa Kahare (Ndugĩre's wife); Ngigĩ wa Mwangi/Gĩthiga wa Mwaũra (Kĩgũũnda); Wanjirũ wa Ngigĩ na Njeeri wa Kamoonjo (Wangeci, Kĩgũũnda's wife); Mang'ara wa Gĩkonyo/Ngigĩ wa Kaguũra (drunkard); Njeeri wa Mũirũrĩ/Njaambi wa Mũirũrĩ (Gathoni); Kamau wa Wakaba (Gĩcaamba); Wairimũ wa Mbũrũ/Lucy Wangũi Hinga (Njooki, Gĩcaamba's wife); Mĩrũrũ wa Kĩarii/Kang'ethe wa Waciira (Security); Johana N. Kang'angi (Mbooi). (On the banning, see Joseph, 2004.)

1982, University of Zimbabwe, dir. Stephen Chifunyise, Ngũgĩ wa Mĩrii and Robert McLaren, *I Will Marry/Ndicharoorwa Kana Ndoda*, toured to Masvingo and Gweru. (Continuing evidence of the fertilization of Zimbabwean theatre by Kenyan work.)

1993, University of Namibia and Windhoek College of Education at University of Namibia, dir. Van der Smit.

1993-1994, Kamĩrĩĩthũ Cultural Troup at Sports View Hotel Kasarani, Nairobi, dir. Choru wa Mũirũrĩ assisted by Nyambura Ngũgĩ. Production taken to Kikuyu Country Club, the Kiboko Highway Hotel in Limuru; Red Nova, Kiambu Town; Mombasa, Leisure Village (Kerugoya), Isaac Walton Hotel, Embu, and at the Railways Club and Rift Valley Sports Club (Nakuru), Source: interview with Choru wa Mũirũrĩ, 12 April 14. See The Diary Theatre, '*Ngaahika Ndeenda* by Ngũgĩ wa Thiong'o', *Daily Nation*, Nairobi, 6 October 94.

2000 January – June Cinema Asmara, Eritrea. Translated into Tigrinya by Alemseged Tesfai, dir. Jane Plastow. Sponsored by Eritrean government, the production opened the international conference on African Languages and Literatures, and ran with paying shows at weekends and with free shows for Eritrean high school students. Also televised by ERITV. See Jane Plastow (2005) 'Making Theatre in the Opera House, Asmara, Eritrea', in *Moving Worlds: Postcolonial Cities. Africa*, 132-6. Ngũgĩ described the gathering as 'one of the most incredible conferences I have ever been to' (Sander and Lindfors, 2006: 407). The controversial Asmara Declaration was adopted at the Conference.

2003, May, Breakthrough Art Company, at Citrus Whispers Theatre, Ngara, Nairobi, dir. Conrad Makeni. See Njagi, Anthony, 'Stage Set for Controversial Ngugi's (sic) Play', *Daily Nation*, Nairobi, 25 May 2003.

2004, August, Arts Ablaze Theatre at the Kenya Cultural Centre, dir. Makeni, with John Gatheiya (Ahab Kīoi); Makeni (Kīgūūnda); Eunice Njoroge (Wangeci, Kīgūūnda's wife).

2004, September/October, University of Witwatersrand's School of Arts drama students, dir. Fred Mbogo, Production Manager Genny Higgs; Jeremiah Mntonga (Kīgūūnda); Shuga Motlanthe (Wangeci); Ayanda Khala (Gathoni); Raymond Ngumane (Gīcaamba); Vuyiwa Kshangela (Njooki); Sello Motau (Kīoi); Juanita Azannai (Jezebel); Xolani Zuma (Samuel Ndugīre); Khathochelo Mbanda (Helen). See Abraham, S. Z, 'Kenyan International Student Directs Ngugi Play', *Wits International Students Discussion and Information Forum's* Blog 01 September 2004. (See Mbogo in this volume.)

2007, St. Lawrence Students, See Nuwagaba, Edwin, 'St Lawrence Students Stage Ngugi's play', *The Monitor*, Kampala, 27 July 2007, http;//allafrica.com/com/stories/200707261183.html

2009, May, African and Caribbean Student Association, at International House Assembly Hall, with Nancy Kasvosve (choreographer), See Kasvosve, Nancy, '*I Will Marry When I Want*: Telling our Own Stories', usapglobal.

2012, October, Lusaka Playhouse, dir. Crawford Moyo, producer Kebby Mwansa, cast Ndugire: James Chishala (Helen); Phenny Walubita (Kīoī); Dominic Sitamu (Jezebel); Gift Muneka (Drunk and Choir Leader); Michael Ziba (Wangeci); Musonda Kasoma (Gathoni); Rachel Katiba (Kīgūūnda). See 'Lusaka Playhouse Revels in Ngugi's Play', beste http;//zedchronicle.com/?p=22, 15 September 2012.

Maitū Njugīra/ Mother Sing for Me, 1982

In her book and in his thesis, Bjørkman (1989) and Joseph (2004) scrutinize the process by which this play evolved. In Sander and Lindfors's volume (2006: 157-9), Ngũgĩ speaks for himself of his role in collecting songs and of the 'active collaborative effort' that went into the production. He also refers to the impact on his role of the fact that the piece was set in the past, that dialogue was limited and that slides were incorporated into the presentation. He defined his participation as being 'more of an editor'. He drew attention to the fact that the people involved were veterans of *I Will Marry* and knew of the political wrath they might incur by participating.

1982, Kamīrīīthū Community Theatre with University of Nairobi's Free Travelling Theatre, Open Rehearsal at Education Theatre. The application for a licence to perform this play at the Kenya National Theatre from February 19 to March 7 was rejected and this meant the play was effectively banned. At a press conference, Ngũgĩ expressed the Kamīrīīthū Theatre Group's 'extreme disappointment and anger at the manner in which the authorities chose to deal with our application for a licence'. (Press Release quoted in full in Bjørkman (1989: 99-101.) See also Muthai, Wahome, 'Licence hitch angers Ngugi,' *Daily*

Nation, 11 March 1982 also quoted in Bjørkman. See Mũgo interview with Choru wa Mũirũrĩ (12 April 2014.)
1994, Kamĩrĩĩthũ Cultural Troupe, dir. Mũirũrĩ, with Nyambura Ngũgĩ, Kerugoya and Nakuru. (See Mũgo interview with Mũirũrĩ, 12 April 2014.)

The River Between (dramatization of novel) and Matigari 1977
Kapsabet Boys, dir. W. Were, Kenya National Drama Festival. (Source: interview with Were, Wasambo, Lecturer Kenyatta University, 10 March 2014.)
Particularly when it was a set book in Kenya Secondary Schools (2009-2013), the novel was adapted and performed by various groups. See, for example, Jicho Four Productions ('Ambassadors of Theatre for Education'); Fanaka Arts put on a dramatization in 2011, at the Kenya National Theatre, dir. Jasper Odak. Also put on by Starlight Productions at All Kenya's County Headquarters, dir. Morrison Njenga, with Johnson Chege (Waiyaki); Bilal Wanjau (Joshua); Robert Agoro (Kabonyi); Irene Tata (Miriam); Joyce Njenga (Nyambura); Akinyi Muthoni (Elizabeth); Willy Mwangi (Cege); James Maithya (Kamau); Easter Macharia (Kinuthia), (Source: Mũgo interview with Morrison Njenga, 9 April 2014.)
This entry draws attention to the use of Ngũgĩ's prose fiction as the basis for performance and for shared experience. Ngũgĩ has spoken about gifted performers giving public readings of his novels and, significantly, *Matigari* is addressed to the Reader or Listener (Ngũgĩ 1987: 9). Also see Ngũgĩ (1986: 82-5), and F. Odun Balogun (1995), '*Matigari*: An African Novel as Oral Narrative Performance', in *Oral Tradition*, 1: 129-65. http://journal.oraltradition.org/files/articles/10i/10_balogun.pdf. Sander and Lindfors (2006: 121).
As will be recognized, further work is required to research and record the extent, impact and implications of Ngũgĩ 's work in performance.

READING LIST: NGUGI PRODUCTIONS

Primary texts: selected

The Black Hermit, Kampala: Makerere University Press, 1963. Reprinted AWS 51, Nairobi, London, Ibadan: Heinemann Educational Books, 1968.

This Time Tomorrow, Nairobi: East African Literary Bureau (EALB), n.d., probably 1970/1. (Includes plays published earlier *The Rebels* (Penpoint, 11, October 1961: 59-69); *The Wound in the Heart* (Penpoint, 13, October 1962: 23-9) and *This Time Tomorrow*.

—— with Mĩcere Gĩthae Mũgo (1976), *The Trial of Dedan Kimathi*, Nairobi: Heinemann Kenya, and London: Heinemann; Acknowledgements include: '... the play is a result of a collective effort...'

—— with Ngũgĩ wa Mĩriĩ (1980/1982), *Ngaahika Ndeenda*, (*I Will Marry When I Want to*) Nairobi: East African Educational Publishers/ London: Heinemann.

(1981) *Caitaani mũtharaba-inĩ* (*Devil on the Cross*), Nairobi: Heinemann.

(1981) *Detained*, Heinemann, London.

(1986) *Decolonising the Mind: The Politics of Language in African Literature*. Oxford: James Currey; Portsmouth, N.H: Heinemann; and Nairobi: Heinemann Kenya. (Essential essays with pertinent examples.)

(1989) *Statement on* Kenya Government's refusal to grant a stage licence for performance, 10

March 1982. (see Bjørkman, 1989: 99-101).

(1989) *Matigari ma Njiruungi*, (*Matigari*) translated into English by Wangui wa Goro, (1994) London: Heinemann; Trenton NJ: Africa World Press.

'Enactments of Power: The Politics of Performance Space' (1997) *The Drama Review*, 41, 3: 11-30. (One of several relevant essays.)

(2006) *Ngũgĩ wa Thiong'o Speaks*, Interviews edited by Reinhard Sander and Bernth Lindfors, Oxford: James Currey; Trenton NJ: Africa World Press; Nairobi: EAEP, 445 pages. (Interviews span the period from 1964 to 2003, and provide invaluable resource for Ngũgĩ's comments on a very wide range of topics.)

Other sources

Byam, L D. (1999) *Community in Motion, Theatre for Development in Africa*, London: Bergin and Garvey.

Bjørkman, Ingrid (1989) *Mother Sing for Me: People's Theatre in Kenya*. London: Zed Books. (Crucial, scrupulous and detailed analysis of the background to the play, the creative process by which it was 'generated' and the 'rehearsals'. Includes Ngũgĩ's statement of 10 March 1982).

Joseph, Christopher Odhiambo. *Theatre for Development in Kenya*, PhD Thesis, University of Stellenbosch, 2004. Available on line. Includes valuable analysis of Ngũgĩ's ideas in relation to various concepts of Theatre for Development, and to theorists and practitioners such as Augusto Boal and Paulo Freire. Joseph notes that the performance of *Kĩmathi* allowed little or no scope for meaningful participation.

Kidd, Ross (1982) 'Popular Theatre and Popular Struggle in Kenya. The Story of the Kamiriithu Community and Educational Cultural Centre', *Theatrework*, September / October, 47-61.

Gĩchingiri Ndĩgĩrĩgĩ (1999) 'The Kenyan Theatre after Kamiriithu', *The Drama Review*, 43: 2, 72-93.

—— (2007) *Ngũgĩs wa Thiong'o's Drama and the Kamĩrĩĩthũ Popular Theatre Experiment*, Trenton NJ: Africa World Press.

Cantalupo, Charles, (ed.), (1995) *Ngũgĩ wa Thiong'o: Texts and Contexts*. Trenton NJ: Africa World Press.

Sicherman, Carol (1989) *Ngugi wa Thiong'o: A Bibliography of Primary and Secondary Sources, 1957-1987*. London: Zell. (Invaluable resource)

—— (1995) 'Ngũgĩ's British Education', in Charles Cantalupo (ed.) *Ngũgĩ wa Thiong'o: Texts and Contexts*, Trenton NJ: Africa World Press.

Smit, V. D. 'Ngugi wa Thiong'o and the Kenyan Theatre in Focus', M.A Thesis, University of Namibia, 2007. (As the title suggests, an overview of Ngũgĩ's work in the theatre. Available on line.)

Were, Wasambo, CV on line indicates his extensive experience as director, commentator and adjudicator. http://www.ku.ac.ke/schools/humanities/images/stories/docs/WASAMBO_WERE.pdf

The Making of *The Trial of Dedan Kīmathi* by Ngũgĩ wa Thiong'o & Mīcere Gīthae Mũgo at the University of California, Irvine

KETU H. KATRAK

Ketu Katrak offers a personal record of a major production of The Trial of Dedan Kīmathi *at the University of California, Irvine. She describes the process of creating the production, the contribution of Prof. Ngũgĩ wa Thiong'o (UCI) and Mīcere Gīthae Mũgo, to the experience, and the response of student actors and the audience. This is a graphic description of a rare production of one of the major works of modern African theatre.* (Eds)

> The stage was on fire as the British *askaris* stoically defended the British colonial policy of dehumanizing and subjugating the African, and the African, led by the brave Kīmathi, courageously fought back against the colonial evil. At the centre of this heated battle is the question of man's liberty, freedom and independence. Such are universal principles that man holds dear anywhere in the world.
>
> Although the drama is based on the Kenyans' struggle against British colonialism in the fifties by distinguished Prof. Ngũgĩ Wa Thiong'o (UCI) and Mīcere Gīthae Mũgo, this is a universal narrative that the UCI drama students staged with impeccable precision and dedication.
>
> As a Kenyan whose family was directly and adversely affected by the struggle, I was personally and deeply moved by the entire play that often ceases to be a play on stage and becomes in my mind, the actual pain and struggle that my family members had to endure. I know now that sometimes one has to fight for what is already his.
>
> Njoroge Njau [1]

Incarceration, control of bodies, military and police power during British colonialism in Kenya pervade the script and the highly successful production, the United States premiere of Ngũgĩ wa Thiong'o and Mīcere Gīthae Mũgo's co-authored play, *The Trial of Dedan Kīmathi* (8-16 March 2014) at the University of California, Irvine.[2] Ngũgĩ is our treasured colleague, Distinguished Professor of English and Comparative Literature at the University of California, Irvine and by undertaking this production we honour him as a playwright. He was most gracious in participating in the entire process of the production from assisting student-actors during the table work, to regaling us with stories from his personal experience of living through Kenya's difficult history, to

Fig. 1 Oge Agulue as Kīmathi with projected image on the wall; The Trial of Dedan Kīmathi at the xmpl theatre, University of California, Irvine. (Figures 1-6 all taken during the last two technical dress rehearsals (5 and 6 March 2014: © and reproduced by kind permission of Paul Kennedy)

imbuing us with his optimistic spirit of resistance expressed via Kiswahili and Gĩkũyũ freedom songs. This play's remarkable co-playwright, Mĩcere Gĩthae Mũgo also participated in the process of rehearsals and we were graced by her presence (from her position as Meredith Professor for Teaching Excellence in the Department of African American Studies at Syracuse University) for the opening night on 8 March 2014.

After four days of intense table work in late January 2014, and six weeks of rehearsal, going through the rigours and challenges of any production with its small and large crises, the play was ready for an audience. Its unique staging and presentation begins even before the spectators enter the performance area. The lobby itself, of the 'xmpl' (experimental) theatre evokes a prison setting with ominous sounds of clanging chains and keys, heavy footsteps, and the visual presence of stern faced *askaris* – Kenyan soldiers, known as the King's African Rifles (KAR) loyal to British colonizers – in khaki shorts, red fez hats, and guns mounted on their shoulders. Many spectators giggle nervously, trying to diffuse the tension; the soldiers remain impassive and threatening. The spectators submit tickets and enter a dark area where they face a guard before a metal gate. Two or three at a time are allowed to enter a narrow corridor with images of Kīmathi and other historical scenes of the Kenyan anti-colonial struggle. The spectators are trapped in this confined space as armed soldiers confront them, staring them down, and finally letting them pass through another metal gate that clangs loudly behind them. Even for spectators who may be familiar with the play, this creative and unique entrance, inducting them into prison for the next two and a half hours, evokes a jarring reality of the control of one's body and will by the colonial prison system with armed guards. As an audience member, Professor Manuel Goméz, UCI's Vice-Chancellor for Student Affairs (now retired), commented:

> From the moment I walked through the jail doors, hearing the deathly slamming sound, I entered into an extraordinarily creative, emotional, historical wallop to all my senses . . . no, an assault on my heart and consciousness, and at the end, I wobbled out still in bone silent emotional contortions. (email, 10 March 2014 to the production's choreographer, Professor Sheron Wray, Dance Department, UCI)

As the audience finally enters the performance area and notes the chairs arranged in the round, their eyes catch the centre where the play's hero, Dedan Kīmathi, hands and feet chained, sits on a raised podium behind bars. Oge Agulue, UCI's Master of Fine Arts student who played this particular Kīmathi, was masterful in his interpretation of the role: his energy and passion moved many audience members to tears. Ngũgĩ noted that Oge Agulue was the best Kīmathi he has seen. Kīmathi remains in his jail cell, chained, behind bars throughout the show, silently witnessing the action even when he is not in a scene. Even during the intermission, he remains in character. A cast member brings him water in a tin cup replicating prison conditions. As Mumbi Ngũgĩ in the audience conveys astutely: 'How powerfully Oge portrayed the inner and outer struggle of this global hero, who so nobly refused to be awed in the face of the power of the colonial sovereign – by the literal and metaphysical "chains of its body politic"' (email to Katrak, 9 March 2014). Although Kīmathi in the play is in a literal prison, for Ngũgĩ and Mũgo, all people living under oppression, or under neo-colonial leaders are equally incarcerated, mentally and psychologically.

The action begins in the Courtroom: White Judge Henderson, in a charade of 'justice', reads out the charge. The time is 1956 during the dark days of the British-imposed Emergency (1952–1960). Martial law fills the atmosphere with terror for ordinary Kenyans. 'Sudden darkness . . . Distant drums grow louder and louder.' Dominated unfairly, ordinary people resist their oppression as expressed in their raised voices in song. From behind the wings, first softly and gradually gaining in strength and energy, the audience hears the words of a freedom song:

Tutanyakua
Masamba yetu
Tupiganie
Uhuru wetu

Translated by Ngũgĩ:
We shall take back our land
We shall liberate our soil

Fig. 2 Ensemble members as chained slaves: Anthony Cloyd, Jessica Mason, Nia-Amina Minor, Maribel Martinez, Jennifer Jones, with black slave trader played by Blake Morris (© Paul Kennedy 2014)

Live drumming by Anindo Marshall and Tom Mcnally (from Los Angeles, brought into our production by our choreographer Sheron Wray) accompanies the song. The actors emerge singing and dancing this song that asserts that the land belongs to the people, and that this soil will be liberated from foreigners. They chant: 'Away with Oppression. Unchain the People.' As the play's co-author, Mīcere Gīthae Mūgo reminds us: 'the deliberate use of Kenyan/African orature was to affirm the creativity of the masses. In African orature, song and dance are important mobilization tools that liberation struggles have used to great effect' (email to Katrak, 5 May 2014). A loud gunshot interrupts the song as the villagers scatter. Our attention is drawn to a dramatized pageant of 'Black people's history' (*Trial*, 4), where an African slave trader sells chained humans to a white slave buyer. The play throws the audience into the brutal past, recreating slaves' inhumane treatment in captivity with sounds of whiplashes and screams. Through skilful lighting, four such scenarios are depicted using movement, stylized and expressive dance choreographed by our faculty colleague, talented choreographer, Sheron Wray. As the play's co-author, Mīcere Gīthae Mūgo notes most usefully (email to Katrak, 5 May 2014):

> The evocation of 'slavery' as a theme historically connects various forms of imperialist enslavement under settler colonialism in Kenya (and continental Africa) to the Middle Passage and the Trans-Atlantic Slave Trade. It is an important *Sankofa* moment with critical symbolic linkages to the Pan Africanist and Internationalist sites: a reminder that imperialist domination and oppression against Black (and other dominated people) go centuries back.

These effective portrayals immediately implicate the audience as witnesses, not as distant spectators to this nightmare of human history unfolding at close quarters as they sit at the edge of their chairs. The play's director, Dr Jaye Austin Williams (Visiting Assistant Professor at UCI) staged the action evocatively, not only in the round, but took this further as dancers and actors moved between the rows of chairs, often making direct eye contact with the spectators, at times, brushing them with their costumes, and indeed, their very breath. This performance 'presents a unique opportunity' comments Dr Williams in her Director's Note in the programme, 'to confront roundly (i.e. in the sense-surround) the violent meld of Transatlantic Slavery and African Colonization'. Njoroge Njau notes: 'Many thanks go to the director, Jaye Austin Williams for wonderful and great work that no doubt took time, energy, effort and dedication to bring to fruition.'

As director Dr Jaye (as we fondly called her) notes, the play 'meditates on what a trial would have looked like if justice had actually been carried out. It's a series of four trials that play out in the mind of this legendary figure.'[3] At the outset, in the Courtroom the white Judge Henderson, who also plays the prosecutor, the 'friend/enemy of the African people', emerges from the bowels of the stage in his full legal regalia complete with a wig, reciting the charge that is repeated over and over again in the play. Kīmathi is in custody ironically enough not for being the leader of an armed guerilla struggle but on a technicality, namely that he was found 'at or near Ihururu in possession of a firearm, namely a revolver which under Special Emergency Regulations constitutes a criminal offence. Guilty or not guilty?' Ngũgĩ notes (email to Director Williams, 14 February 2014) that

> all the courtroom speakers are aware of the audience around them in the courtroom and by extension the actual audience in the auditorium who can be seen as an extension of the courtroom. So, some of Kīmathi's words and even the Settler's are direct appeals to their followers as if the crowd/the public is the real judge/real jury. There are two sets of judges in the courtroom: the Judge himself and the public. The Kīmathi sequence leading to the 'unchain my soul' is addressed to the public jury. So also are the settler's words: 'I had a wife and a daughter. My property. Where are they now?' (*Trial*, 29)

The play portrays a cast of Kenyan revolutionaries who support Kīmathi– Woman, symbolic of all working mothers with tenacious commitment to Kenya's liberation, and ordinary Kenyans. A young Boy and Girl, deeply influenced by the Woman, represent the nation's youth who will direct its future. The Boy and Girl are significant 'as youth' notes the play's co-author Mīcere Gīthae Mūgo, 'who take on the baton in the race against colonial oppression and neo-colonial treachery' (email to Katrak, 5 May 2014). There are also 'hooded collaborators' who betray their own people, literally hiding behind hoods and pointing out the Kenyan fighters to the British for arrest.

The play powerfully and affectively portrays the injustices endured by ordinary Kenyans during the period of Emergency imposed mainly to destroy the Mau Mau struggle headed by leaders such as Dedan Kīmathi. As Ngũgĩ comments in a local newspaper article: 'To see the struggle that (the protagonist) had to go through, fighting against the British Empire still near its height, that's a David-versus-Goliath story, and that kind of message and struggle is always relevant.'[4]

Kīmathi faces 'four trials' in his jail cell. He sees through every 'trick'

Fig. 3 Girl played by Sakina Ibrahim (© Paul Kennedy 2014)

Fig. 4 Girl and Boy: Sakina Ibrahim as Girl and Anthony Cloyd as Boy (© Paul Kennedy 2014)

The Making of The Trial of Dedan Kīmathi

Fig. 5 Jacob Dresch as Colonial officer tormenting an ordinary villager, a fruit seller, played by Blake Morris, and a hooded collaborator played by Daniel Song in the background (© Paul Kennedy 2014)

Fig. 6 Oge Agulue as Kīmathi being visited in his cell by the Judge Ian Henderson played by Matt Koenig (© Paul Kennedy 2014)

Fig. 7 The cast and creative team of The Trial of Dedan Kīmathi *at the xmpl theatre, University of California, Irvine, Opening Night, 8 March 2014. Centre, Oge Agulue as Dedan Kīmathi; to her left, the co-authors, Ngũgĩ wa Thiong'o and Mĩcere Gĩthae Mũgo (© Ketu H. Katrak 2014)*

presented to him by Henderson who visits him twice – once to be conciliatory, offering to 'spare' Kīmathi's life if he would call off the fighting in the forests, and when he cannot break him, to order that Kīmathi be tortured. Next, neo-colonial politicians and bankers visit Kīmathi in his cell – European, Asian, and African – whose capitalist purpose overrides their racial identity. Co-opted black politicians, 'neo-slaves', 'black skins and colonial settler's hearts', 'drinkers of blood' as Kīmathi calls them only spout the colonizers' line about giving up the armed struggle, of working towards independence by getting a few seats in the Legislative Council, lured by sitting around 'conference tables in London', getting shares in motor companies, and other bribes of wealth and power. The co-author, Mĩcere Gĩthae Mũgo's interpretive comment is astute, namely that the Banker, Politician and Priest are 'the representatives of the institutions of the superstructure under capitalism. The kind of "freedom" they offer Kīmathi all foreshadows current oppressive conditions under neo-liberalism' that continue in Kenya today (email to Katrak, 5 May 2014). The reality of the masses of destitute Kenyans, portrayed in the play, with many still fighting in the forests to reclaim their land are entirely left out of these discussions on 'Partnership in Progress'. They have also missed out on getting the 'English education' that becomes key to success after independence.

The Trial of Dedan Kīmathi masterfully portrays different segments of these co-opted Africans – the KAR African soldiers who fought for their colonial masters during World War II and who continue to serve the *mzungu* (whites) in Kenya, controlling and killing their own fellow Kenyans. A crucial moral

The Making of The Trial of Dedan Kīmathi   85

Fig. 8   Centre, Oge Agulue as Dedan Kīmathi, with co-authors Ngũgĩ wa Thiong'o and Mĩcere Gĩthae Mũgo (© Ketu H. Katrak 2014)

Fig. 9   Centre, Ketu H. Katrak (dramaturg) with co-authors Ngũgĩ wa Thiong'o and Mĩcere Gĩthae Mũgo (© Ketu H. Katrak 2014)

dilemma confronts Kīmathi in his flashback to the forest when he is faced with his own brother Wambararia who has now become a collaborator with the British. Should Kīmathi order that his kindred brother be killed since he is a traitor to their cause? He is torn and he cannot order his brother's murder. In this vacillation, this great leader, as the Woman narrates to the Boy and Girl, was 'too human'.

The play ends on a positive note of continuing struggle with ordinary 'workers and peasants singing a thunderous freedom song':

> Tutapigana mpaka mwisho
> Tufuge vita na tutashinda
> Majembe juu mapanga juu
> Tujikomboe tujenge upya
>
> Translated by Ngũgĩ:
> We shall fight for our land,
> We shall fight and succeed.
> We liberate ourselves.
> We build a new society

Both Ngũgĩ and his wife Njeeri wa Ngũgĩ assisted us with pronunciation and melodies of the freedom songs in the play in Gĩkũyũ (Ngũgĩ's mother-tongue) and Kiswahili. Again, Njoroge Njau voices what Ngũgĩ told me is 'a people's endorsement' of our production. Njau continues:

> I was greatly impressed, in particular, by their dedication and the hard work they had put in the mastery of the play and understanding of the culture, history and the people they played on the stage. They were pronouncing with ease names of people and places that I know they could only have been so articulate through a sustained effort and commitment to the task. I salute you all for your stellar performance.

The power of this production and the successful embodiment of Kenyan history and culture by young students in the Department of Drama was a team effort by the director, choreographer, dramaturg, and the design team working on sound, lighting, costume, and stage-management under faculty mentors. The planning stages began in fall 2013 for the play opening in March 2014. The students received high praise from none other than the Kenyan community in the audience who valued the validation of seeing their own history depicted with such sensitivity and thought. As Njoroge Njau remarks:

> Kenyans who came to see the play have given glowing tributes of the beautiful work that UCI drama students did in executing the play. Many have even confessed that they really hadn't grasped properly the pain and anguish our people had endured in order to free our beautiful country from the yoke of colonialism. Indeed, they were grateful for a renewed lesson in their own history.
>
> Kenyans in Diaspora are immensely thankful and indebted to all the UCI drama students for telling our story. We are full of praise to you and wish somehow you will have a chance to go to Kenya and visit with the people you so proudly presented on stage. Now, you too are children of our struggle. Since you have felt the weight and price of the struggle, you no doubt know the value of freedom.

History and its discontents

The student performers along with the design and creative team of *The Trial of Dedan Kīmathi* prepared to enter the colonial world of Kenya in the 1950s with its atmosphere of fear, threat, arrests of entire villages, fear of detentions at the whim of colonial officers, by reading a packet of materials compiled by myself as dramaturg along with two assistant dramaturgs, doctoral students in the Department of Drama, Allison Rotstein and Sonia Desai. The readings included classic essays on colonialism, neo-colonialism, race, culture by Frantz Fanon, Ngũgĩ wa Thiong'o, Mĩcere Gĩthae Mũgo, Orlando Patterson, theoretical readings on slavery, on Black being, British propaganda about Kīmathi including a documentary that we screened as part of our four-day intense table work.[5] We provided the readings to the cast and creative team as a 'gift' for the holidays in December 2013, so that by the time work began in January they were equipped with some basic information on colonialism, and Kenya's history.

Our purpose in sharing these materials with the actors and creative team was to layer their understanding of the play, to grasp its *political purpose*. We aimed to equip the actors to take the next challenge of inhabiting these ideas in their bodies as they enacted their roles on stage. The director, Dr Jaye who has worked as a Literary Dramaturg, welcomed this engagement of ideas with actors and designers.

Ngũgĩ himself attended all four days and enlightened the students with many fine insights into interpreting the text, and historical details of the colonial situation in Kenya from his own research and life experience. He told us that this is a very personal play for him and that although he has published many novels, and volumes of essays, including his recent memoirs, drama has had the most impact on his life. It was, after all, his co-written play, *I Will Marry When I Want* (with Ngũgĩ wa Mĩriĩ) at Kamĩrĩĩthũ community centre with collaboration from local peasants and workers on the script, production, including building a 2,000 seat theatre, that proved so threatening to the Kenyan State under Jomo Kenyatta that Ngũgĩ was imprisoned for a whole year (1977-78) at Kamĩtĩ Maximum security prison. During his long days in prison, he recognized the power of using not English but the peasants' local language, and telling the stories significant to their lives. Ngũgĩ also asserted to the students that physical incarceration, difficult as it undoubtedly is, did not imprison his imagination; hence, he managed to write his first Gĩkũyũ novel, *Caitaani mũtharaba-inĩ* (later translated in English as *Devil on the Cross*) on toilet paper while in prison.

Ngũgĩ explained to the students that the play primarily explores the relationship, and often the disjuncture, between law and justice, and that such issues are still with us. He asked whether one can have justice under criminal laws such as during colonial times, and more recently, under Florida's 'Stand Your Ground' law that freed the white perpetrator of the cold-blooded murder of unarmed black teenager Trevon Martin? The production ended with the freedom song by the ensemble and then as the stage went to black, the projected images on the walls included dark renderings of 'justice' to blacks in the US – Rodney King, beaten brutally by Los Angeles police officers (2 March 1991) whose unconscionable acquittal led to the Los Angeles Riots, and more recently (26 February 2012) the unarmed teenager Trevon Martin, shot by a white murderer supposedly 'standing his ground' in Florida.

Ngũgĩ shared the daily threat that Kenyans faced under the British and the specific fight over land in Kenya since this became a settler colony where the whites appropriated the best land, dispossessed the indigenous owners of the fertile Highland (renaming them the White Highlands) and forced the local people to labour on the land for the colonizers' profit. Much of this history was new for the student-actors.

Further, it was important for the actors to understand that although the play takes us into the heart of this segment of Kenyan history during the British imposed Emergency (1952–1960), it recreates an imaginative history as in what might have transpired if the British had actually held a trial for Kĩmathi. As a black man, he is already guilty before the trial even begins. Ngũgĩ and Mũgo excavate a misrepresented segment of Kenyan history, reconstructing it imaginatively, even resurrecting Dedan Kĩmathi as a hero of the Kenyan people, disrupting British propagated negative myths about Kĩmathi.

A central exchange about law and justice takes place between Judge Henderson enacting the charade of 'even-handed justice', and Kĩmathi's challenge to the lie that 'There is only one law, one justice'. Rather, Kĩmathi retorts that there are 'Two laws. Two justices. One law and one justice protects the man of property, the man of wealth, the foreign exploiter. Another law, another justice, silences the poor, the hungry, our people' (25-26).

Ngũgĩ pointed out to the students that since Kenya was the first among the African colonies to confront the British via an armed struggle, the colonizers were determined to denigrate the movement as inhuman, as driven by primitive oath-taking ceremonies, by barbaric killing sprees, all of which totally belied the organization and discipline of the Kenya Land and Freedom Army led by charismatic figures such as Dedan Kĩmathi. If the armed resistance succeeded in Kenya, this would be a dangerous precedent for other British colonies. Indeed, in a battle over naming, the British misnamed the struggle as Mau Mau indicating mumbo jumbo pervaded by dark deeds and motives. The Mau Mau put a high price on loyalty, inducting members into the movement through a secret oath ritual. The British were hell-bent to get these oaths out of the captured Mau Mau; the ones who were captured were taken to 'reeducation camps', often subjected to physical and psychological torture. Throughout the struggle, the British lost less than 100, whereas 11,000 Mau Mau were killed. Along with physical killings, the British demonized Mau Mau as terrorists; hence Kenyans themselves, especially the neo-colonial elite who came to power after independence, despised the movement as demonic and wanted to wipe it out. The British colonial tactic of divide and rule effectively divided Kenyans who were loyal to the British from their kinsmen belonging to the Mau Mau.

The Making of The Trial of Dedan Kīmathi

Ngũgĩ narrated a personal incident when he and Mĩcere Gĩthae Mũgo, both colleagues at the University of Nairobi in 1971, saw a play with completely false and negative portrayals of Kīmathi. As they left the theatre, they both felt compelled to write a play correcting these falsehoods, and indeed they felt responsible to 'resurrect Kīmathi' as Ngũgĩ noted in our table work, from such disparaging myths. As they note in their Preface to the text:

> There was no single historical work written by a Kenyan telling of the grandeur of the heroic struggle of Kenyan people fighting foreign forces of exploitation and domination . . . We agreed to co-author a play on Kīmathi . . . a hero of the Kenyan masses.

Ngũgĩ himself enjoyed the entire process of the table work, and then rehearsals, always providing useful insights though never overtly interfering with the director's vision. I was often the scribe keeping notes and then sharing them with the director, assistant director, and choreographer. Everyone had the highest respect for Ngũgĩ and valued his views enormously. I was deeply heartened to hear from Ngũgĩ's wife Njeeri that this entire experience of working on the play's production had inspired a light-hearted buoyancy in Ngũgĩ making him feel ten years younger. Indeed, whenever I met with him to talk about the play, he would express an infectious excitement. He is always the most patient and generous teacher, addressing any questions or concerns from the young actors for whom the fabric of this play, initially foreign and distant, became through the process of a true educational experience, very close to their own hearts. Ngũgĩ himself feels like the team has become his family and he shares with them the events and honours that he continues to receive in his distinguished life.[6]

The Drama Department generously hosted Mĩcere Gĩthae Mũgo who joined us (with her daughter Mumbi wa Mũgo) from Syracuse University for the Opening Night. And before that, with the use of modern technology, Mĩcere Gĩthae Mũgo was with us via skype on the first day of our table work. As we traversed the rehearsal hall, to listen to the presentations by the set designers, then the costume designers, and so on, Mĩcere on the laptop accompanied us and looked into the scenery and the costumes and also entered our hearts with her words of encouragement. Both she and Ngũgĩ at that first memorable session reminisced about the time over 40 years back when, as colleagues at the University of Nairobi, they had agreed to write a play together on Kīmathi, 'to set the record straight' to use Chinua Achebe's well-known phrase upon the publication of his classic first novel, *Things Fall Apart*. Later, Mĩcere Gĩthae Mũgo was present for the final dress rehearsal when she provided key insights to the student who played the Woman – a role that Mĩcere herself had played many years back. She contributed significantly to an interview/conversation with Ngũgĩ that was filmed for a documentary on 'The Making of *The Trial of Dedan Kīmathi* at UCI', and for our celebratory Opening Night. Ngũgĩ and Mũgo succeed in what they note in the Preface to the play as 'the challenge to truly depict the masses (symbolized by Kīmathi) in the only historically correct perspective: positively, heroically, and as the true makers of history.'

My personal journey to the production of *The Trial of Dedan Kīmathi*

The idea of having the Department of Drama undertake a production of one of Ngũgĩ's plays was a dream of mine that I kept filed away in my mind for many years. Ngũgĩ and I have been colleagues at UCI since 2002 when he joined the University of California, Irvine, as the Inaugural Director of the International Center for Writing and Translation. We had talked often about doing one of his plays on campus. In 2013-2014, the time was right for the Department of Drama to undertake this project. At UCI, in 2013, Ngũgĩ was awarded the University's highest honour, namely the UCI Medal. He had already been nominated twice for the Nobel Prize in Literature along with receiving ten honorary doctorates from institutions worldwide over the years and many other honours. Among these accolades, none had specifically honoured Ngũgĩ as a playwright. Our production of *Trial* aimed to recognize his work in this area.

The Department of Drama's annual season usually includes six full productions that are selected via a democratic process involving input and discussion by the department faculty, especially those involved in the acting and design aspects of production. As a member of the doctoral faculty in the Department, I also had an interest in the practical aspects of theatre making, particularly as a dramaturg where I could combine my scholarly skills with the realities of production. I had served as dramaturg at one of the most prominent regional theatres in the United States – the Oregon Shakespeare Festival (OSF) – when their Artistic Director, Bill Rauch, had invited me to be the dramaturg for OSF's production of the ancient Sanskrit play, *The Little Clay Cart*. I could not have had a better location to learn both the skills required of a dramaturg, and the realities of production.

The theme of the annual season of plays selected in 2013-14 by the Department of Drama was 'justice'. Perfect, I thought to myself. *The Trial of Dedan Kīmathi* was concerned centrally about law and justice, indeed 'two laws, two justices' as Kīmathi resolutely declares in the court during his imagined trial. One law protects the wealthy, and another law is served out to the poor and destitute. Issues of injustice, of the haves and have-nots, of the struggles of ethnic minorities in many of the inner cities of the United States all made this play a relevant choice for production.

I presented, tentatively at first, my idea of doing Ngũgĩ's play at the Department of Drama's Season planning meeting in March 2013. Our Department Chair, Professor Gary Busby and other faculty came on board as the idea of honouring Ngũgĩ as a playwright was very appealing. Further, the prospect of this production facilitating connections between our Department and Humanities and even beyond to other Schools, was deeply appealing.

In a historic gesture uniting a large segment of our campus, *The Trial of Dedan Kīmathi*, was co-sponsored by Deans of the Schools of Arts, Humanities,

Social Sciences, Social Ecology, and Law. Ngũgĩ had expressed a desire to have a professionally made film of the production and we managed to get funding for that along with making a documentary film, 'On the Making of *The Trial of Dedan Kĩmathi* at UCI' from our Provost, Professor Howard Gillman, and University Extension. The documentary – including table work with actors, Ngũgĩ, and the creative team, rehearsal shots, interviews with the co-authors – will showcase our work in time for UCI's 50th year celebrations in 2014-2015.[7]

Let me end with a few testimonials from audience members who were deeply moved by this production. One of our first year doctoral students, Anna Renee Hansen wrote to me in an email (23 March 2014):

> I am so glad that UCI is putting on such important, relevant plays. It made me feel very proud to be a part of this program. The show was moving, powerful, and thought-provoking – everything theatre should be in my estimation! The most powerful part for me was the Brechtian audience involvement, the way we couldn't escape – we were implicated in our spectatorship. It was uncomfortable, maddening, entertaining, heartbreaking, beautiful. I know you and your team worked very hard on it and I want to thank you for everything you did to make this production so excellent.

Dr John Daly, Assistant Vice Chancellor for Human Resources at UCI commented in an email to Njeeri wa Ngũgĩ (9 March 2014):

> Never did I feel immersed in a play [as I did watching *Trial*]. Tonight I felt like a participant . . . I wanted to get up from my seat and free Kĩmathi from his chains. I wanted to grab a gun from one of the British soldiers. I was completely caught up in the moment. It became live theatre to me and not a play . . . The actors were amazing. You would never know they were college students in Irvine! They completely made me believe they were citizens of Kenya in the 1950's.

Another spectator whom I had invited, 90-year-old, prominent Japanese-American author, Mitsuye Yamada, one who had undergone incarceration (along with 110,000 Japanese-Americans during World War II in the US) remarked (email to Katrak, 10 March 2014):

> I want to congratulate you for this enormous success of a play where everything, from the language, the music, the acting, and the presentation all came together in such a stunning way! I've never seen a play where I was completely drawn in emotionally in the first few minutes and kept on this emotional intensity throughout (until the intermission). At the same time, there were so many intertwining political and social issues I felt as though my heart (or brain?) would burst!

Finally, Kenyan Njoroge Njau, whose words began this personal reflection, are equally fitting to end with. I could not have hoped for a stronger 'people's endorsement' as Ngũgĩ noted to me, of our efforts than Njau's words:

> This, our story is now yours as well. Thank you.
> And thanks to one and all organizers and contributors including The University of California, Irvine (UCI) for giving a voice to our people who fought so courageously; not for a price or recognition but for human freedom and dignity.

NOTES

1 Njoroge Njau sent this via email (17 April 2014) to Ngũgĩ who shared it with the cast and creative team. Njau was an audience member along with others from the Kenyan community who attended the production of *The Trial of Dedan Kīmathi*, at the University of California, Irvine (UCI). Njau and others travelled nearly three hours by car from Bakersfield to Irvine (around 150 miles) to see this play.
2 Ngũgĩ wa Thiong'o and Mĩcere Gĩthae Mũgo (2006) *The Trial of Dedan Kīmathi*, Nairobi, Kampala, Dar es Salaam: East African Educational Publishers, Ltd. First pub. 1976. Published in USA (2014) by Waveland Press, Inc: Long Grove Ill).
3 Director Williams quoted in Joel Beers, 'Ngũgĩ Wa Thiong'o Is the Lion in Exile', *OC [Orange County] Register*, 3 March 2014, 5.
4 Ngũgĩ quoted in Joel Beers, 'Ngũgĩ Wa Thiong'o Is the Lion in Exile', *OC [Orange County] Weekly*, 6 March 2014, Arts page.
5 Some of the readings in the packet were from Frantz Fanon (1961) *The Wretched of the Earth*, trans. R. Philcox, NY: Grove Press, Repr., 2004; from Ngũgĩ wa Thiong'o (1981) *Decolonising the Mind: The Politics of Language in African Literature*, London: Heinemann, and *Globalectics: Theory and the Politics of Knowing*, New York: Columbia University Press, (2012); from Mĩcere Gĩthae Mũgo 'Art, Artists and the Flowering of Pan-Africana Liberated Zones', Mwalimu Julius Nyerere Distinguished Lecture, 2012 (Dar es Salaam: University of Dar es Salaam, 2013); Mĩcere Gĩthae Mũgo (2012) *Speaking and Writing from the Heart of My Mind: Selected Essays and Speeches*, Trenton NJ/London: Africa World Press; British Colonial Office (1960) *Historical Survey of the Origins and Growth of Mau Mau*, Presented to Parliament by the Secretary of State for the Colonies by Command of Her Majesty, May 1960 (London: Her Majesty's Stationery Office); Ian Henderson and Philip Goodhart (1958) *The Hunt for Kīmathi*, London: Hamish Hamilton; Donald L. Barnett and Karari Njama (1966) *Mau Mau from Within: Autobiography and Analysis of Kenya's Peasant Revolt*, New York and London: Monthly Review Press; Orlando Patterson (1982) *Slavery and Social Death: A Comparative Study*, Cambridge MA and London: Harvard University Press.
6 Recently, Ngũgĩ wa Thiong'o was elected to the American Academy of Arts and Sciences, a well-deserved honour.
7 For the third consecutive year, UC Irvine was ranked first among US universities under 50 years old by *Times Higher Education*.

A Rain of Stones
A Play for Radio

First broadcast on BBC Radio 4, 7th January, 2002.
Cast: Dr Meklis: Patrice Naiambana; Dedau/Sekumi: Madhav Sharma; Risela: Priyanga Elan; Hezra: Rashid Karapiet. Directed by Pauline Harris.

WOLE SOYINKA

CHARACTERS
Dr. MEKLIS   *Archeologist*
RISELA   *His Assistant, daughter to Hezra*
SEKUMI   *An old family retainer*
HEZRA   *Guardian of the Scroll*
DEDAU   *City Elder*

Dedicated to the Memory of the Algerian Writer

TAHAR DJAOUT

and all other victims of Religious Zealotry

A Rain of Stones

Music from a portable cd player. Sound of pick and shovel. Scraping. An archeological dig is in progress. A sharp increase in the tempo of scraping and displacement of pebbles, accompanied by heavy, excited breathing.

Pause, during which the music is heard more clearly – oriental music – raga or similar mode.

The sound of a small shovel dropped, then softer sounds as bare hands take over and earth is brushed aside.

Meklis [*Intense, barely suppressed excitement*] Pass me the brush.
Risela It's in your pocket, Dr. Tekilis
Meklis Oh, so it is, excuse me.
Risela You think...?
Meklis Without a doubt. Without one iota of doubt.
Risela I ... think so too. I can hardly stop myself shouting *Eureka!*
Meklis [*Soft Strokes of Brushing*] You may, but not shout, Risela. Just whisper it.
Risela [*Softly*] Eureka. [*Laughter*] I feel better. I would have burst otherwise.
Meklis Lend me a hand.
Risela Oh yes, it is heavy.
Meklis Feather light, considering the weight of history that rests on it. In that sense, it's heavier than the tons of earth that have hidden it from sight these thousands of years.
Risela [*Sudden excitment*] Doctor!
Meklis What is it?
Risela Look down, Dr. Meklis. No, you'll have to put your eye right against the crack. Here, take my place. Lie flat. [*Sounds of scrambling*] I could see the edges of several more, going straight down. They appear to reach all the way down to the bottom – can you see?
Meklis Yes, yes....The torch, Risela. Bring the torch. [*Rapid strides*] No, you keep hold of it. I spotted one other crack – over there to my right. Place it against the crack. [*Pause. Gasp*] Oh my god!
Risela You can see them?
Meklis Right down to the bottom.
Risela It's similar to steps left by well diggers. Only much neater and regular than one would expect.
Meklis Just like this one. It's clever. Really clever. They have indeed been embedded to simulate stone steps. And I suspect they're all emplaced just like this first one. With the inscripted side facing downwards – to protect the writing.
Risela You think it's a shaft, a natural shaft? Or was it deliberately dug up?
Meklis I think, when we've thoroughly excavated, we'll find it is a well. Man-made. In those days, they did not dig steps into the sides but used chunks of stone, sticking out just like those. Oh, no question, it's a disused well. Only, instead of storing water, it's...its...it's words. Words of faith cast in stone. A series of simple book shelves, only delving downwards instead of ascending. Book shelves, literally. Very literally. The book shelf as its own text. [*Chuckles*]

Risela You've done it doctor. Congratulations.
Meklis We've done it Risela. Oh God! It's like....no, nothing like this since that goatherd stumbled on the the Dead Sea Scrolls in a cave.
Risela I was going to say, doctor, I mean, I can only think...imagine if the Upanishads had been lost for a thousand years, and were then found by a peasant in a cave in the Himalayan mountains. Or a goatherd stumbling on fragments of the stone tablets of the original Ten Commandments....
Meklis You mean, the ones supposedly smashed by an angry Moses?
Risela I was fantasizing, trying to imagine a comparable find to this....
Meklis Well Risela, if that tale is true, those fragments may yet be found. Why not?
Risela Dr. Meklis, don't tell me you're already dreaming of your next excavation!
Meklis It would be an anti-climax but – no, I take that back. Uncovering any form of physical evidence that brings real life to a tale, a legend, any fragment of oral history, brings with it its own unique feeling. Each find is a universe, a micro-universe of creativity and – sometimes, sadly – vanished ingenuity. So who knows, we may still come to tackle that but...no, objectively, it could never compare to what I think – no, what I would swear with my entire reputation – those slabs will prove to be, those stone testaments jutting out from the wall below us. The Pure Mentor, Shafez predated Moses by nearly three millennia. This, this is truly... [*Meklis blows his nose, overwhelmed*] Damnit! All this dust...
Risela [*Softly*] That's all right doctor, I understand.
Meklis Twenty-three years....
Risela It's all over. You are vindicated.
Meklis We've merely uncovered the tip of the iceberg. [*Again, his chuckle*] What a most discordant expression, considering we're dealing with rocks and soil, not frozen water. And yet, most appropriate, most appropriate. We are, after all, standing on its very tip of a submerged bookshelf – I shall restrain myself and avoid saying – library. Although, who knows...? Oh, I'm beginning to get carried away. Still, if we find nothing but this one tablet, even if those other steps are clean, prove to be nothing but bare rock, no inscriptions whatever like this...
[*Sound of feet scrambling down an incline. earth and pebbles cascading down.*]
Meklis Who is it? We've grown careless. Quickly. Cover up that opening while I haul this into the main chamber.
Risela It's only Sekumi.
Meklis Ah, his timing is perfect. If anyone is entitled to share this moment...
[*The scrambling feet come to an abrupt stop*]
Meklis [*Mock rebuke*] Tst-tst-tst-tst, Sekumi. You have abandoned your post.
[**Sekumi** *responds with dumb sounds, excited.*]
Risela Yes, we found it Sekumi, just as Dr. Meklis predicted. And of course, thanks to you and your memory.
Meklis Well, you certainly move fast for an eighty-year old man! I would have sworn it was one of Dedau's scouts...

[*Noises from* **Sekumi**]
Risela It seems an excitement of this kind is no respecter of age, doctor. I seem to recall that you were yourself – er – somewhat overcome a few moments ago.
Meklis That was just the dust...
Risela Of course, of course. I forgot all about the dust. [*They both laugh*]
Meklis And now Sekumi, lend Risela a hand and stuff up this indentation – it's much too conspicuous. Anyone can see that something with a distinct shape – a well manicured slab if I may so describe it – has been eased out of the side. Join me in the workshop chamber. We'll continue in there to distract prying eyes, while we think of the next step. The euphoria is over. We must pull ourselves back to the present.
[*Boots retreating rapidly, noise of shovel at work, plus* **Sekumi's** *excited 'speech' sounds.*]
Risela Yes, that should do it. I hope no one saw you leaping down into the pit – for all the world like a mountain goat – at your age, Uncle! They might suspect that something was afoot. [*Sounds from Sekumi*]. The summons to evening prayers have been sounded? All right then. Our secret is still safe. Let's join the Doctor.
[*Crunch of boots fading off. Distant sound of a gong. Fade in* **Dr. Meklis**.]
Meklis [*Slight echo, indicative of a cavernous space.*] I'm over here. Come on in. [*Footsteps*] Sekumi, stay at the entrance and keep watch.
Risela Oh, we needn't worry. The gong has already struck the hour of noon prayers.
Meklis Which provides one of Dedau's spies a perfect excuse to stroll over. Your father's companion is a thorough man. He doesn't let prayers get in the way of his snooping.
Risela I must admit you're right, doctor. Sekumi...
[*Retreating footsteps*]
Meklis [*Sighs*] Pity we haven't a bottle of champagne we could pop – and not just in celebration. My throat is all clogged with dust. Ah well, pass the thermos and we'll celebrate with cups of your mint tea. After which, I insist you take off and get some rest while I bring our logbook up to date.
Risela [*Laughs*] Come on, doctor, I know why you wish to get rid of us. You are going to start work on the translation.
Meklis We-e-e-ll, yes. Yes. By tomorrow morning we must reveal our find to the Council – and of course to the world. And who knows what that will bring? Tonight – tonight at least is mine. I must know what this first tablet has to say to me, this ancient, long abandoned script. A clue, at least, just a glimmer of what else lies below. I won't get any sleep otherwise.
Risela Take more than one night, doctor. Take a week if you like. Sekumi knows how to keep a secret.
Meklis Poor Sekumi....but, no Risela. It would almost amount to a breach of trust – I am thinking of your father of course, and of that contentious evening at his dinner table.

Risela We could bring him into the secret...
Meklis And leave Elder Dedau out? Your father would never agree to that. Dedau may be a raging fanatic but he is still your father's friend – and confidant. I studied him closely during that dinner – an unbending, unforgiving type.
Risela All right, doctor. A quick toast then. [*Sound of liquid being poured.*] Here you are. [*Another pouring sound.*] So, here's to you, doctor.
Meklis To knowledge, Risela. To knowledge and – Truth.
Risela Yes, to Truth, at last. [*Pause*]. Good night, doctor.
Meklis Good night, and – thank you.
[*Retreating footsteps. Fade into dinner table sounds.*]
Hezra Truth, doctor, truth? Come, come, no one here is afraid of Truth. You're merely trying to provoke Elder Dedau.
Meklis Well, only partially. But I do ask you, since you are the theologian of The Faith, suppose we do discover...?
Hezra Not suppose, Dr. Meklis. When. Because you will. It is down there in the Holy Spot, and you will find it. That virtually uninhabited part of the city outskirts was not named the Holy Spot for nothing.
Meklis You should have let me conclude, Guardian Hezra. We shall find the tablets, there I agree with you. But suppose, when we've deciphered those Scriptures, we find in them passages that contradict some tenets of the Faith...
Dedau The doctor surely states a most improbable thing.
Hezra Improbable? I would say impossible. The extant Scriptures in the Scroll are clear. Quite unambiguous. They make constant reference to the Twenty-one Precepts of the Prophet Shafez. Our religious observances have been based strictly on those precepts.
Meklis Yes, the Twenty-one Steps to Illumination. But the scrolls are products of later theologians. They were transmitted orally, and were not set down on parchment until ... 5 millennia after the birth of the Prophet Shafez? Those scrolls....
Dedau Scroll, Dr. Meklis, the Scroll.
Meklis But there is more than one.
Dedau The Scroll is the name by which they are known. That they are written on several pieces of parchments, by many hands, and preserved separately means nothing. They are One Scroll, indivisible.
Meklis Allow me to continue. The Scroll – if you wish – was based on oral transmission, and it is on account of the same oral tradition that the seventh, ninth, fourteenth and seventeenth steps have remained objects of controversy, thanks to the very proliferation of copies. The veracity of those four precepts is disputed.
Hezra By sceptics, Meklis.
Dedau By heretics. And where are they today?
Hezra They've mostly died off, I would say. Some were killed of course.
Dedau They died the death of heretics.
Meklis [*Sighs*] It really is a pity that the annual tradition of the public recital was ever abolished. The audiences served, in effect, as witnesses to authenticity or deviation.

Hezra I regret it myself. It appears to have been a great festivity, a celebration also of the rhetorical arts. Twenty-one prime bulls were slaughtered, feeding the entire populace. There was music and dancing all day, with the most colourful masquerades on parade.

Dedau It could only have been a heathen spectacle. A corruption of the Faith by practices held over from the old religion, in fact a revival of paganism masquerading under celebration of the Faith. Thank goodness it was abolished.

Hezra Let's not confuse the facts, Dedau – the Festival of the Precepts was abolished because a branch of the original band of followers of the Mentor Shafez began to exploit it as an occasion to challenge The Scroll. They persisted in their versions of the four – er, well – heretical precepts. Quite a cantankerous lot, it seems – [*Laughs*] I have developed a rather soft spot for them – and their times – from what we have since learnt of them.

Dedau Guardian Hezra is much too indulgent towards those vipers! The Scroll has stood the test of time. Five millennia after the birth of our prophet and seer, the Pure Mentor Shafez, it continues to serve as the spiritual beacon for our people. Even the doctor agrees that the Faith is the oldest written religion in the world.

Meklis The evidence is overwhelming. And in any case, carbon-dating will confirm it beyond all doubt whenever the tablets are found. I have staked my reputation on that.

Dedau And it has preserved its founding purity. No schisms. No sects. The Pure Mentor Shafez has been vindicated. His sufferings, his matyrdom under the futile rampage of King Taklima

Meklis Speaking of King Taklima's role in this history, Elder Hezra, tell me, what's your view – frankly now – on the story of how the tablets were saved?

Hezra Ah yes, The Day of the Rain of Stones. For the majority of us, a day to celebrate the triumph of the Faith and the death of the old superstitions.

Meklis Yes, superstitions now. But at the time, it was the state religion.

Hezra So it was, until Mentor Shafez received divine guidance, broke from the old ways and revealed his Twenty-one precepts. His servant, Adarusa, set them down in stone tablets. King Taklima was enraged. He not only supervised the smashing of the tablets, he had every particle gathered up and placed in fibre baskets. With his retinue at his heels, he climbed the peak of Mountain Kosra....

Meklis The place of execution.

Hezra Yes, the spot from which felons, traitors and heretics were flung into the void, and with his own hands, King Taklima hurled the baskets one by one into the void. He wanted to ensure, literally, that not one fragment of a word survived to link up with another.

Meklis But his daughter had already saved the day, unknown to him?

Hezra Risela is revered today as the patron saint of the Faith. [*Chuckles*] A brave woman – I named my daughter after her. She had already secretly converted and she could preempt all the court's efforts to destroy the Faith.

Meklis So, you accept the Sidramun version?

Hezra It is extremely plausible. According to Sidramun, twenty-one tablatures were indeed smashed, yes, but it was not the real tablets that fell to the king's iconoclastic rage. Risela commissioned the making of a false set of tablets. They were duly cut, polished and inscribed. The Preceptors – the Mentor's disciples – then agreed that if any of them were caught by the king's agents, he should not even wait to be tortured to reveal the hiding place of the fake tablets.

Meklis And so, Elder Hezra, no one knows what the authentic tablets really contain. No one can vouch for the precepts on which the Faith is based today.

Dedau The authority of the Scroll remains infallible. And its predictions will surely come to pass.

Meklis Predictions? Such as?

Dedau Of course you are not privileged to consult the Scroll. You are not of The Faith.

Hezra Among its predictions is that, after that first, there will come two more days of the rain of stones. And that the third shall witness the destruction of the world.

Meklis It would seem most religions feel incomplete without some apocalyptic vision.

Dedau The Scroll has survived fires and floods. It has earned the crown of eternal validity.

Meklis Even more than the tablets?

Dedau How do we know those exist for certain! We have only these contradictory versions to go on. King Taklima could very well have laid his hands on the authentic tablets and destroyed them. It is so far-fetched, this notion that a mere woman like the Princess Risela could have plotted to make false copies of the tablets for her father to destroy. It is beyond belief.

Meklis Assuming that you're right, the four crucial precepts remain in contention.

Dedau They are not the four legs of this dining table. The table of The Faith has other supports, durable as Time.

Meklis Elder Hezra, can I ask.... ? Are we speaking freely?

Hezra *[Chuckling]* Dr. Meklis, Forget that you're sandwiched between two City Elders, one of them a Guardian This is a completely affable, after-dinner exchange among seekers after truth.

Meklis I am digging for the truth – literally. We shall find the tablets, Elder. But what happens afterwards, that remains crucial for me. Will it prove the beginning of illumination? Or are we headed for another day of the rain of stones? Will it, this time also? Are we going to have another orgy of smashed tablets? I would like some form of guarantee.

Dedau You have permission to dig. Why should the Council offer you anything else?

Meklis The Scroll is at least two thousand years younger than the tablets. Memory is not a frozen template, immune from the erosion of time. Now suppose...

Dedau The Council has given you permission to dig, and that's the end of the matter.
Meklis You do understand. I have not spent these many years on frustrating research only to provide the occasion for another rain of stones?
Dedau For an archeologist, you certainly tend to the dramatic.
Meklis Do I?
Hezra Your apprehension is unfounded, doctor. My daughter Risela is determined to dig alongside you, she's determined to bring her namesake's work to light. And I'll lend you my old retainer, Sekumi – you'll find him also indispensable in more ways than one. At last, we stand poised to know the truth...
[*An electric buzz*]
Come in Sekumi. Yes, you may clear up, thank you, and serve coffee – mint tea for the doctor. Tomorrow, you will join Risela and Dr. Meklis at the site and keep his workers in line.
[*Sound of plates being cleared. Otherwise, silence.*]
Hezra Do say good-evening to our guests.
[***Sekumi's** speech sounds*]
Hezra The last upheaval of the Faith took place nearly seventy years ago. Sekumi is the sole surviving casualty of the last family that was still regarded as being of the Preceptor line. There he is, a testament to the insanity of that holy – or more accurately – unholy war.
[*Followed immediately by the sound of opening door, then the soft pad of feet.*]
Meklis How did it happen?
Dedau They pulled out his tongue – from the roots. It's a miracle that he survived.
Meklis But why? Why?
Hezra [*A brief pause*] We do not know. However, his entire family – his parents, grandparents, were killed. There is no question – they were singled out for total elimination by an extremist sect, fortunately now more or less wiped out. Their belief was that Sekumi's family had knowledge of the hiding place of the missing tablets. You see, when we speak of martyrs, it is no abstraction with us.
[*Pause*]
Meklis In our work, we encounter much evidence of the glories of religion, but even more of its savagery, reminders of its propensity for tyrannising and destroying.
Dedau Dr. Meklis if I had a choice, your licence would be rescinded.
Hezra Dedau!
Dedau I hold my peace.
Hezra Elder Dedau, Dr. Meklis has his permit already – it will not be withdrawn.
Meklis Thank you, Elder Hezra.
Hezra Ah, here comes Sekumi with the tray.
[*Music*]
[*Soft footsteps*]

Meklis Who is it? Sekumi? Who's there?
[*Approaching footsteps, steady, coming closer... Pause*]
Meklis Who is it? Come closer. Don't be afraid.
Dedau [*Nasty chuckle*] Please, Dr. Meklis, do turn that torch away from my face.
Meklis Oh you, Elder Dedau. Isn't it late for you to be prowling around an excavation site. It is not very safe. Come to think of it, shouldn't you be at the prayer ground at this hour.
[*Footsteps forward. The stone tablet is lifted.*]
Dedau [*A mocking laugh*] I know these grounds better than you do, Dr. Meklis.
[*Pause. Footsteps forward. Stop.*]
The Guardian was right. If anyone could uncover the tablets, you would.
Meklis How did you know?
Dedau Oh really, doctor. I thought you much cleverer than that. Did you really think I had withdrawn my eyes from your activities altogether? Not in the least. You could almost say that I shared your discovery with you – the very moment that you made it.
Meklis I see. I would never have thought that you would descend to eavesdropping. But since you have, you know that I was about to embark on deciphering this ancient script. It's going to be a prolonged business and I would like to put in a few hours before bedtime.
Dedau Really. And to what purpose may I ask?
Meklis What is that supposed to mean?
Dedau To what end? Why? What should it matter to you – what has been safely and peacefully buried these past five thousand years and more?
Meklis Why are you so nervous? I have yet to translate one damned word.
Dedau Or excavate the thousands and thousands of words on the tablets jutting from the walls of the shaft – I know that, Dr. Meklis. I know that. That's why you're here. That is why you abandoned the comforts of the world of infidels to come and breathe the arid dust of our city. You are searching for something to fulfil yourself, to earn a reputation in the world. The famous Dr. Meklis who uncovered the five thousand year old tablets, repository of the teaching of a neglected seer and prophet, first of the Holy Men.
Meklis The oldest recorded religion in the world, yes. It shatters the claims of these other much-vaunted world religions, puts them in their place. Isn't that something that you should take pride in?
Dedau Pride is emptiness of soul. The Scroll is sufficient testament to the unmatched antiquity of the teachings of Shafez.
Meklis But the Scroll proves nothing absolute. It is barely two thousand years old. The tablets, on the other hand...
Dedau The tablets are superfluous. And they may undermine the authority of the Scrolls.
Meklis It is the four controversial precepts that worry you?
Dedau [*Pause*] We would like you to leave the country, Dr. Meklis.
Meklis With my task barely begun? And who are 'we', Dedau? Does that by any chance include Guardian Hezra...

Dedau Guardian Hezra is what he has always been – a vain man who places the adventures of the mind above the sanctity of the soul. He has been my friend from childhood, so I know him well. He prides himself on an openness – which really is a sign of weakness. It's like opening your chest to the cold wind, Dr. Meklis saying that you wish to test the many degrees and tempers of the wind. Of course you catch a cold. That is the weakness of Guardian Hezra. He has never understood when to shut the door against the cold wind.

Meklis And you of course, have spent your life doing nothing but keeping that door firmly shut.

Dedau The injunctions of the Scroll are clear Doctor. *Let not the vanity of a curious mind bring death to the innocent, or destruction to the Faith.*

Meklis I am a man sifting through the debris of history to find where truth is lodged. I have no intention of taking issue with you and only ask you to let me alone to get on with my job.

Dedau [*Sighs*] Have you seen the rest of the tablets?

Meklis A glimpse, no more.

Dedau Would you like to see them?

Meklis Like to see them? I intend to excavate them.

Dedau How soon do you intend to tackle that?

Meklis Tomorrow morning, first thing. I doubt if I'll be able to get any sleep tonight.

Dedau Would you like to *see* them? Touch the rest of them. Step on the rungs of the ladder they form down the well. *Descend the steps to illumination....*I quote from the Scroll...*The pathway to illumination is not always ascent, but descent on the steps of the precepts.* Now, would you like to see them?

Meklis You mean right this moment?

Dedau You see, Dr. Meklis. I solved that riddle long before you. It must be humiliating to you to learn this now, but I have been there. I explored the Holy Spot myself. I am not without a little strain of curiosity you know, and I have the advantage of knowing the Scroll. There were clues in the Scroll, scattered all over its pages. They began to add up. And I found the secret way down – no, not through here. From this chamber, you'd really have to dig. But just outside, yes, beside that reddish boulder...

Meklis You found it? You've been down the well?

Dedau Several times, but never all the way down to the bottom. I wasn't inclined to have them cave in on me, oh no. That would be divine retribution for an unholy curiosity. And anyway, for what? I lack the skills to translate the ancient script. And I am neither a Preceptor nor Guardian. So I would have desecrated a place of sanctity – purely for my own vanity. Indeed, I felt I had already gone too far. Such considerations do not matter to you of course, so, come. I'll show you. I've sent word to Risela to join us.

Meklis Oh, that was most thoughtful. As thoughtful as letting us dig and scratch for two thirds of a year, knowing very well where the tablets were buried!

Dedau Yes, your activities did fill my days and nights with the deepest thoughts. Such as – how much time do men waste seeking what already is, what has been and will remain for all time? You were the perfect vindication of the doctrine of total submission to the authority of the Scroll.

Meklis I am not sure what you really are Dedau. A simple fanatic? A sadist? Or a combination of both.

Dedau Don't be bitter, doctor. I know I've robbed you of what should have been the great moment of your life. An epiphany, no less. But at least you did 'discover' something. I missed that first tablet after all. The side-shaft through which I made my entry appears to have gone under it – maybe it was embedded too close to the roofing. But come... Bring the torch, Dr. Meklis, let us shed some light on this world of darkness – isn't that, after all, what you're after?

[*Fade in voice of* **Risela**]

Risela But why, Sekumi, why should he leave without a word? I mean, without a direct word to us? Why use a messenger? And to you? Was this what he really had in mind when he urged us to take a break and leave him alone? Virtually pushed us off the site? He wanted to leave the country?

[**Sekumi** *makes noises*]

Oh? You don't think he sent the message? Who then?...... Dedau? Of course, Dedau! I'm glad you agree. It's that scheming primitive, he and his squad of thugs, the so-called Purity Vigilantes...So what do we do now? We've got to stop them, Sekumi, we've got to stop them before they reach the border....All right, let's find father. Wait! Oh no!

[*Pause*]

Risela The timing! Is that just an accident? What? [*Really agitated noises from* **Sekumi**] You think it was no accident?...You think he knew? He knew we'd found the tablets?... But how, Sekumi, how? How could he have known? There were just you and I, no one else? Did you spot any of his spies when we left? We've got to find father and stop them at the border. No? What else could we do? Go to the site? You think he's still there? But the message you've just given me ... oh, you think Dr. Meklis would have left a note at the site? Some kind of sign? It makes sense, yes, that makes sense. Dr. Meklis is a most resourceful man. All right. To the site then – no, let's split forces. I head for the site and look for that note, or sign. You go and find father. Bring him over directly, but tell him to send some of his men to head them off at the border....

[*Fade off. Fade in voice of* **Meklis**, *echoing from a deep well,* **Dedau's** *is normal. He is on the rim of the well.*]

Meklis [*Awed voice*] It's sublime, Dedau, it is simply sublime down here. And solid. Not the slightest danger of caving in. You should have ventured all the way down.

Dedau It was not important. It sufficed that mine were the first feet in millennia to touch those tablets. I trod the footsteps formed of the teachings of the Pure Mentor. I was blessed above all living beings. That was enough.

Meklis I do not, I cannot understand how anyone could stop halfway. How? You actually stopped and explored no further?

Dedau I retreated at the seventh step.

Meklis But what were your thoughts, Dedau? Did you feel – as I do? That this spot is the womb of thought, of spirituality itself? What did they think of, the First Preceptors who so loyally embedded these tablets down the wall. And what shall we find, when we eventually decipher these writings? Wait ... wait a minute. Dedau! Did you know there was a tunnel down here?
Dedau What tunnel?
Meklis Wait a minute. I am looking at more than one tunnel, Dedau. I am looking at two...no, three tunnels... leading off this central shaft. Oh, this is incredible. It is not just tunnels – wait ... after two or three meters, they widen into chambers, underground chambers. Oh, my god!
Dedau Speak up Meklis. I cannot hear you.
Meklis [*Awed whisper*] The vaulting. The vaulting alone. Oh god, god, god, who were these people? What was the nature of faith that created this wonder?
Dedau Chambers? Did you say chambers?
[*Quick returning steps at the bottom*]
Meklis [*Raised voice*] Yes, I did say chambers: radiating from the central shaft.
Dedau I didn't know there were chambers.
Meklis Because you did not come all the way down. They're flush with the floor of the well. You wouldn't notice them unless you stood on the floor.
Dedau [*More to himself*] I never... descended beyond...the seventh step.
Meklis Come down Dedau. You have to. You have to see for yourself. You won't believe what I am looking at here, what is making me tremble. Look, even the light is wobbling – that's because my hands are unsteady.
Dedau I can no longer hear you.
Meklis [*Shouting*] I said, you won't believe what is down here. I need someone else to see it, tell me I am not hallucinating. Or am I? Does excessive depth play havoc with one's senses? Maybe there are magnetic forces underground which create these images. I mean, is there such a thing as depth drunkenness? It's possible... mirages may also form at certain depths below earth....
Dedau What's that? What else is there?
Meklis The vaulting, Dedau. The lining of the vaults.
Dedau Yes?
Meklis Epiphany!
Dedau What did you say?
Meklis Yes – epiphany. How right you were, though yours was said in the spirit of mockery. I'm going back in the chambers, before the batteries run out. Yes, Dedau ... [*Changing acoustics*] More tablets, even more refined, have been used as broad tiles to roof the vaults, and the roofing reaches halfway down the sides. They gleam like yellow filaments of light. The encryption is gold, pure gold. Gold tracing on black basalt – yes, either polished basalt or marble. Dedau, I am looking at illuminated scripts used as vault lining....
Dedau What are you saying? Are you saying there are more tablets?
Meklis [*More to himself*] Countless, Dedau, numberless. Embossed sheets of stone, almost seamless. It's endless. One passage simply leads to another, and then another. It's a maze, an ordered maze, and it needs no expert eye to see

at once that it conforms to some grand design. What design?

Dedau That's where you come in, Mr. Meklis. There is no further mission in life for you – just this. Literally, you have undertaken the task of a lifetime. I can't hear you, Meklis. Your voice is coming over all garbled. Are you saying there are more chambers?

Meklis [*His voice is sad*] No, you cannot hear anything, that's right. You never did learn to listen. Truth will always sound garbled to you, Dedau. Suddenly the four contested precepts fade into nothing. Absolute nothingness. Here I am, walking in the very heart, coursing the very veins and arteries of unparalleled beauty and creativity. While others rampaged, tortured, killed and mutilated above ground, they attempted to immortalise their faith with this wonderous skill, with patient affirmation that the mind can touch the sublime, and the hand the elusive. Oh, I should have brought my recorder. And the camera. Risela must come down and photograph it all....

[*Sudden thud*]

What the...!

[*Rapid footsteps towards the source of sound, voice change to earlier acoustics.*]

Oh, thanks Dedau. Are you a mind-reader? I was just wishing I had my recorder. And camera. But – damnit! [*Sounds of rummaging*] [*Shouts, really angry*] Dedau, have you gone mad? What made you place the tablet in the bag?

Dedau I thought you might want to compare it with the others while you're down there.

Meklis You are a true primitive. You've smashed it in pieces, with all my equipment.

Dedau Did you say there were more chambers?

Meklis [*Growling*] An endless network – chambers and galleries. For all I know, it extends for miles. Look, come down and see for yourself. Now you've destroyed what I strongly suspect was the index. Oh, thank goodness – it broke in clean pieces. We'll put it together, but it won't ever regain the condition of its companions.

Dedau And tablets? Any more tablets?

Meklis Come down and see for yourself, damn you! We've no sooner stumbled on the eighth wonder of the world than you begin to destroy it. The Eighth Wonder of the World...

Meklis And all of it over four thousand years old, could be even between five and six thousand. The steps are a mere teaser – but a major problem. They've been embedded just like the first – with the encrypted side underneath – but you know that already. We must first ease them out one by one, study the writings on them and replace them with identical slabs, to recreate the approach to the chambers. That's what we'll do. The tablets should be brought to the surface where the whole world can see them. No one in his right mind would wish to displace the vaulting of course – that would be unthinkable. But the steps, yes, I think we can legitimately bring those to the surface, maybe recreate the stairway above ground, with the encryption facing up...

[*Sound of knuckle on shale. A muted musical sound.*]

Hm. Quite a musical ring to it. [*Again, strikes the tablet*] Wait. My bag ... at least the hammer would have survived ... yes, the hammer. Some kind of commentary in that I suppose. Camera gone, tape recorder in little bits, computer pulverised but – the hammer survives. That's the way it goes. Brute partners – religion and hammer ... Still ... yes, here it is. Now, let's see what we have.
[*Strikes the first slab. The note is clearer.*]
Meklis I thought so. Remarkable vibration for such a thick slab of stone ...
[*Strikes another – pause – another*]
I wonder... May yet prove to be nothing but – I do wonder...*Tam...tam...tam...* Can't reach the next from here – up, Meklis ...*tam...tam...tam...tam...Tam...* oh- oh. Starting all over again? Maybe just a coincidence. We'll soon find out. Up we go...*tam...tam...tam...tam...tam...tam... tam...*And now what? No! No more surprises for tonight please, my heart couldn't stand it – *Tam...*! Yes, back to the tonic – because that's what it is – another full scale! And I bet those remaining seven steps...of the twenty-one – well, might as well put it to the test. Here goes *Tam...tam...tam...tam... tam...tam...* and I need no outside opinion to tell me that the final tablet, now lying below in pieces, would also have been – back to the tonic. Three sets of a scale. Figure Three and Figure Seven. Any significance? Wait a minute – the three tunnels below? Is that it? No, musn't read too much into these things but, one does seem to echo the other. Seems to re-so-nate! Could be a guide to what else lies hidden in those galleries? It must mean – *something!* Why else take the trouble to construct a stairway in three scales of seven notes each!

Dedau [*Voice very close by*] You seem to be enjoying yourself, Dr. Meklis.

Meklis Oh! you startled me.

Dedau Don't blame me. You forgot I was here. Making more discoveries, I see.

Meklis You really *should* come down. It's one thing after another. I can tell I'm going to spend months here. Years. An eternity. Did you hear all that just now?

Dedau Hear what, Dr. Meklis, hear what?

Meklis [*Strikes the last note again, again and again – tam-tam-tam-tam-tam-tam!*] These 'steps to illumination', these hand-carved stones of shale or basalt or whatever – I'm no longer certain, no longer sure of anything – they were actually arranged as a musical scale, descending and ascending. [*Sighs*] But to what purpose? What do they mean? Where do they lead?

Dedau I thought you said they do lead into some underground chambers.

Meklis [*Groans*] Serve me right for bothering to talk to you.

Dedau I have to leave you, I'm afraid.

Meklis Oh? Well, I suppose I should also tear myself away from it all – for now. All the equipment is smashed. Nothing more I can do tonight. I'd best come with you. Oh, you did say Risela was on her way, didn't you?

Dedau Yes. She'll be thrilled to learn of your new find.. You come up with something new every moment. Take your time, Dr. Meklis.

Meklis Not as much as I would like to take. The batteries of this torch will soon give out. I'll wait for Risela above ground. My pathetic – source of light is no match for this cave of illuminations.

Dedau I think you'll find it more than adequate for your needs. If you look in the bag, you'll find a spare set of batteries. That should provide you a few more hours to roam the chambers and galleries. Or catacombs. All by yourself. Risela says you love nothing more than to be by yourself with your ... discoveries.

Meklis [*Chuckles*] True, true. She is perceptive.

Dedau I'll let her know you appreciate her.

Meklis I shall tell her myself....

Dedau I don't think you'll be able to, Dr. Meklis. And if I were you, I would move away from where you now stand and into one of those chambers – they should form air pockets where you can explore to your heart's content – well, for a few more hours anyway. Maybe a whole day. Even a week.

Meklis What was that you said?

Dedau I give you full joy of your – epiphany.

[*A cascade of rocks, pebbles and sand.*]

Meklis What the...!

[*A groan. A prolonged cascade, then the distinct sound of small pebbles bouncing off hard surfaces, tunefully. Silence. Then running footsteps. Panting.*]

Risela Dr. Meklis....Dr. Meklis...

Hezra Dedau! What's going on here?

Dedau I am not sure myself. I came looking for Meklis but the site appears deserted..

Hezra You haven't seen Meklis at all?

Dedau No. I received word that the Purity Vigilantes were looking for him. Planned to abduct him and take him over the border. I came to warn him but found no sign of him.

Hezra Are you sure of that?

Dedau Absolutely. I've shouted myself hoarse calling his name.

Risela His bag, all his worktools are gone.

Hezra Then we'd better hurry to the border. We may be in time to stop them.

[*Sounds from* **Sekumi**]

Risela Oh yes, Sekumi. Wait, father. What of the noise we heard on the way here.

Hezra Oh yes, we heard a rumble beneath our feet as we approached, like cascading rocks.

Dedau I am glad you heard it. It did sound like a rockfall. I hesitated to believe the message of my hearing.

Hezra The earth seemed to tremble beneath our feet.

Dedau And just before then, I heard some strange music. It was eerie, evil, clearly satanic.

Hezra [*Impatiently*] Oh come on Dedau. Just for once, why don't you hear something uplifting – like the music of the spheres?

Dedau It seemed to come from the bowels of earth. Of a mode I had never heard before. Dark, unmistakably evil.

Hezra [*Sighs*] Have it your own way. At least we did hear something on which we can both agree – falling rocks. That will do for me.
Dedau It rooted my feet to the spot. Thank goodness you came along at the time. I was petrified out of my senses.
Hezra [*Resignedly*] All right, Dedau. So what did you make of it?
Dedau Do you doubt what it was? It was one thing and one thing only – a rain of stones – the second. We brought this on ourselves ...giving permission for a stranger to tread the venerable grounds of the Preceptors.
Hezra Oh Dedau, we've been through that often enough. Come on Risela, we've wasted enough time here.
[*Footsteps leaving*]
Dedau My friend, my dear brother, leave well alone. If he's gone, he's gone. Excavating in the Holy Spot... I warned you at the time, it was a deed of impiety. But that's all over now. If the Purity Vigilantes have got him and hustled him over the border, there is nothing more we can do.
Risela He knows something. He knows all about this.
Hezra It's obvious. But we'll still see what can be done. Let's go.
Dedau This was the second Rain of stones. Can you deny it? Maybe others have witnessed it, wherever it did take place, but at least we heard it, you and I. We felt it. Remember the prediction. The third Rain shall be the harbinger of the destruction of the world. May it not happen in our lifetime.
Hezra Amen to that, Elder Dedau. Amen.
Risela Are we going or not, father?
Dedau Cursed be the hand, by which the third rain comes along – remember that also, Hezra. Even if it came about in all innocence, his clan is forever accursed.
Risela Are we going to stay here all night?
Hezra Maybe ...maybe we should reconsider this, daughter. Wait till the morning and summon a meeting of the Guardians.
Risela Reconsider? Wait?
Hezra Yes, Risela, I think we should ...act with some prudence, now that things have taken this turn.. Let the Guardians decide. For all we know, the good doctor has already been taken beyond our reach.
Dedau Now you're using your good sense of judgement. Let's all go together. If we leave now, we may yet meet the rest of the faithful at evening prayer.
Hezra Yes. Come Risela.
[*Sounds from **Sekumi***]
Risela On second thoughts, father, I think I'll wait here. With Sekumi. The doctor may yet turn up.
Dedau Spoken like a true child of the Faith. The Scroll teaches us to have faith in miracles. Come Hezra, to prayers.
[*Fade in music beneath a gentle fall of sand.*]

The End

Book Reviews

New Plays from Africa (all available from www.africanbookscollective.com)

Munyaradzi Mawere, *Rain Petitioning and Step Child (Plays)*
Mankon, Bamenda: Langaa Research and Publishing Common Initiative Group, 2013
ISBN 978-9956-790-70-8, £15.95/$19.95

Rain Petitioning and Step Child is a collection of two plays. This first, *Rain Petitioning*, is made up of three scenes and each scene is divided into three stages. Although it has an interesting story, it is not a well-written piece as there is neither dramatic conflict nor character development. The dialogue is for the most part stilted; a fact made worse by many grammatical mistakes, some of this one feels is caused by the dramatist's deployment of a local register and idiomatic expression. Added to its weakness as drama is a lack of sense of the play as a performance piece: it is filled often with unusual stage directions. The second play, *Step Child*, has some dramatic intrigue: the complicated background of Babamunini creates conflict as by custom he is entitled to inherit his biological father's estate but is prevented by tradition from doing so as he had also been prevented from inheriting his step-home. But no resolution is offered in the end, with the play left in mid-action with Babamunini's lament for his double loss. *Step-Child* also suffers from a similar poor use of English and weak character delineation.

Kelvin Ngong Toh, *Fointama: A Play*
Mankon, Bamenda: Langaa Research and Publishing Common Initiative Group, 2013
ISBN 978-9956-791-73-6, np

Fointama is the tragic love story of Fointama, the head of the hunters, and the Princess of Fuli, who naively colludes in him being framed and subsequently hanged for physically abusing the princess. But sub-textually, the play is about corruption in a land in which personal ambition overrides every other consideration and where morality is totally mortgaged to individual needs and schemes. There is a similarity between Kelvin Toh's play and the plays in Bole Butake's *Dance of the Vampires and Six Other Plays* as they are socially engaged plays which, although they use folktales and well-known parables, are concerned with the state of Cameroon. The princess, in love with Fointama and desperately hoping to rid herself of the unwanted love of Ayeah, the Prince of Belo, agrees to a plot to spread the rumour of Fointama's abuse of the princess – an abomination punishable by death – only to see the latter hanged for the rumoured crime. She kills herself and her father, the Fon, also kills himself for his part in the injustice of Fointama's death. Disappointingly though, the real culprits, Ayeah, his father the Chief of Belo, and Fointama's fellow huntsman, Ngoh, who falsely testifies against him, survive.

Bole Butake, *Dance of the Vampires and Six Other Plays*
Mankon, Bamenda: Langaa Research and Publishing Common Initiative Group, 2013
ISBN 978-9956-790-39-5, £24.95/$34.95

Dance of the Vampires and Six Other Plays is a collection that highlights Bole Butake's well-known deployment of his theatre for socio-political commentary; the plays also confirm his status as the foremost Anglophone Cameroonian dramatist of the last two decades. The collection contains prefaces by Francis Wache and Kimeng Hilton Ndukong respectively. The first play, which gives the collection its title, *Dance of the Vampires*, is a socio-satirical allegory that comments on the machinations of power in a fictional African kingdom. The reader is left in no doubt who the absolute monarch, Psaul Roi is: echoes of Cameroon's president-for-life, Paul Biya, whose has been in power since taking over in 1982 abound. In his craze for total power, Psaul Roi abrogates all the traditional checks and balances put in place to stop despotic rulers by getting himself initiated into the cult of the vampires. He of course overreaches himself, to the point of almost exterminating the entire population for protesting against his unjust rule. As with most of Butake's plays, *Dance of the Vampires* takes on the entrenched corruption in the political fabric of the country, but although Psaul Roi is overthrown, his successor is Nformi, Psaul Roi's former general responsible for the massacre and already in collusion with Albino, the mercenary foreigner who has been exploiting the nation.

Family Saga, the second play, explores the theme of social inequality built upon exploitation and oppression. The relationship between two supposed brothers, Kamala and Kamalo, who by all accounts should be equals, but who in the play are the oppressed and the oppressor, illustrates the mechanism of misinformation through which such relationships are established and maintained. The play also exposes the historical nature of such relationships through its exploration of the family history of the brothers. Kamala and Kamalo have the same mother, but different fathers. Kamalo calls himself the brain, while Kamala and his children are the brawn supporting the estate; Kamalo does nothing but enjoy the privilege secured for him by his father. In the end however, he is made to realize his injustice and sins against his blood, repents, and the family come together in unity. The hope of the play, unrealistic as it may seem, is that without oppression there would be no oppressor or oppressed.

Lake God can be considered one of Butake's best plays; it fictionalizes the infamous Lake Nyos – a crater lake which exploded and spewed large clouds of carbon dioxide in 1986 which suffocated humans and livestock in towns and villages around it. Butake uses a traditional explanation – the anger of the Lake god at the refusal of a Christian Fon to carry out the annual sacrifice to the god, in spite of the lake's rumblings and the warnings of the priest of the lake – to lay the blame on the 1986 disaster on the corruption and duplicity of the leadership to address what was a known problem. The play is the tale of a land that consumed itself because its leaders failed in their duty of care for the people and the customs.

In *Betrothal without Libation*, Butake takes a swipe at the prevalent ethnic stereotyping that is causing so much of a problem in many African nations and is thus a threat to national cohesion and identity. The play offers inter-ethnic marriage as one way of eradicating parochial ethnocentric attitudes that prevent citizens of the same country understanding and accepting one another as belonging to one country. In the play, Elisa and Fointam are almost prevented from marrying because of the bigotry on the part of the groom's family; but thanks to Elisa's educated parents' open-minded attitude and Fointam's determination to stand up to his family, the marriage goes ahead, albeit without the customary libation by the groom's father. In the end, reason wins and the ignorance that causes such attitudes is exposed and the success of the marriage and reconciliation between the families points the way forward for the whole country.

Like the preceding plays, *And Palm-wine Will Flow*, set in Ewawa, 'an imaginary fondom in the grassfields', explores the failure of corrupt leadership. It pits Shey Ngong, the chief priest of Nyombom, against the erratic Fon. The visionless and greedy Fon surrounds himself with sycophants who dare not tell him the truth, and he proceeds to pillage the entire community, seizing lands, palm trees and produce by force and generally intimidating everybody. Only Shey Ngong stands up to him, refusing to partake of the endless festivities at the palace, and finally succeeds with the help of the gods to restore power to the people.

The penultimate play, *The Rape of Michelle*, attacks the corrupt judiciary as well as the pervasive moral decadence of a society in which a young unschooled girl competes with her mother for the affections of a client. When Michelle does not get the attention she craves from Mikingdong, she alleges rape, after throwing herself at him. Rufina, her mother, also out for revenge, having also been rejected by Mikingdong reports the alleged rape and Mikingdong is promptly arrested by the police. His stay in the police cell, the process of securing bail for him and his eventual court trial reveal the deep-seated corruption of both the law enforcement officers and the entire judiciary, including the defence lawyer, Zende; it is how much money an individual is able to give that will determine their innocence or guilt. Alarmingly, this situation is not challenged as everybody plays the game.

The last play, *Shoes*, is 'set anywhere in military dictatorship'. The play follows four soldiers on sentry duty who have just been used by the authorities to brutally suppress a people's riot – they killed and destroyed the bodies of the rioters and only shoes are left, which they are guarding. But the soldiers are also becoming restless because they have not been paid their salaries while the generals are looking after themselves; in the end most of the soldiers down their arms to join with the people in the mass uprising which First Soldier tells them will ultimately succeed in overthrowing the dictatorship.

Together, the plays in *Dance of the Vampires* in their respective ways are social satires, anti-establishment, revolutionary, and siding with the common folk against authority, whether it is the traditional authority of the Kwifon and the Fon in *Dance of the Vampires*, *And Palm-wine Will Flow*, and *Lake God*, or the constitutional dictatorship of the generals as in *Shoes*. But they also share with *The Rape of Michelle*, *Betrothal without Libation*, and *Family Saga*, a deep concern for Cameroon which Butake perceives to be bedevilled by a corrupt and despotic leadership and ethnic/tribal bigotry that prevents unity and national identity from developing.

Francis Imbuga, *The Green Cross of Kafira*,
Nairobi, Kenya: Bookmark African Publishers, 2013
ISBN 978-9966-055-39-2, £14.95

The Green Cross of Kafira, with a foreword by Roger Kurtz, is the third of Francis Imbuga's trilogy of Kafira plays, preceeded by *Betrayal in the City* and *Man of Kafira*. The trilogy deals with the 'theme of betrayal of trust', especially by political leaders in postcolonial Africa; these plays are highly critical of the corruption and greed of political leaders, but they also hold out hope for social change. In the play, two agents of government (Serikali), Mwodi and Yuda, meet to discuss how to attack and neutralize the opposition to their power posed by Bishop Ben'sa of the Green Cross of Kafira and Pastor Mgei and Madam Mgei, founder and now leader of the Green Cross Clinic which houses the rejects or dissidents. Pastor Mgei and a few others are in detention for activities deemed to be against the state – the pastor for founding the clinic and Adema for becoming radicalized at university where he was studying for a Masters degree. The metaphor of the clinic as a place of healing is not lost because within its walls the rejects rehearse and eventually perform their freedom which is the freedom of all Kafirans, with the play ending with the elevation of Pastor Mgei as the new leader of Kafira. Thus the optimism of the trilogy is maintained and justified in the end.

Osita Okagbue
Goldsmiths, University of London

Samuel Kasule, *Resistance and Politics in Contemporary East African Theatre: Trends in Ugandan Theatre since 1960*
London: Adonis & Abbey Publishers, 2013
ISBN 9781909112384, np

At the heart of Samuel Kasule's book is a very welcome analysis of the work of Uganda's best known playwrights. Although there are a number of books available about Ugandan culture which include discussion of theatre, notably Eckhard Breitinger's 1999 edited volume, *Uganda; The Cultural Landscape,* as well as a number of useful but unpublished PhDs by such as Rose Mbowa (1994) and Susan Kigali (2004), there has previously been no published book length study of Ugandan theatre in English. Sam Kasule does not attempt to cover every aspect of Ugandan theatre history. His work is particularly strong on the work of the playwrights who to varying degrees, but with considerable popular success, contested the outrageous mis-governance of Uganda under the two regimes of Milton Obote in the 1960s and early 1980s and the disastrous rule of Idi Amin throughout most of the 1970s.

Chapters Three and Four deal with the work of the founding 'fathers' of modern Ugandan theatre: Byron Kawadwa, the first director of the Ugandan National Theatre and Cultural Centre, infamously murdered by Amin's men in 1997; and Wycliff Kiyingi, a pioneer playwright most famous for writing Uganda's longest running radio soap series, *Wokulira*, between 1962 and 2000. The two men had very different approaches. Kawadwa wrote musical plays in Luganda, frequently drawing on history to obliquely critique the state of governance in Uganda, although he also adapted both European (Poquelin's *The Miser*, 1970) and African (Soyinka's *The Trials of Brother Jero*, 1969) playwrights' work for popular Ugandan consumption. Kasule is fascinating in this chapter when he touches on how Amin's Ugandaization programme led to the closing of cinemas which greatly benefited indigenous theatre, while in 1976 'Kawadwa's Kampala City Players had become the unofficial wing of Express Football Club [after the club was forced to close] because of its popular performances of Baganda based plays' (63). I know of nowhere else where the tribulations of football so benefited a theatre organization. Kasule's book is peppered with such contextualizing anecdotes which I only wish had been more substantially discussed so that one could understand better the particular factors to have influenced Ugandan theatre other than the strictly political. By contrast, Wycliff Kiyingi was a graduate of Uganda's premiere, colonially established, boarding school, King's College Budo, which had a strong amateur drama tradition. This led him to set up Uganda's first indigenous theatre organization, the African Dramatic Association, in 1954, to write Uganda's first formal play, *Pio Mberence Kamulali*, in the same year, and to put great emphasis on fully written – as opposed to partially improvised – scripts.

Chapters Five and Six look at the work of a raft of playwrights who benefited from the popularity of theatre under Amin, as one of the only spaces in which often allegorical texts based on Ugandan folklore dared, with varying degrees of covert or overtness, to critique abuses of power. Cliff Lubwa p'Chong gets Chapter Five to himself while Eli Kyeyune, John Ruganda, Nuwa Sentogo and the female playwright Elvania Zirimu share Chapter Six. In Chapter Five Kasule touches on the fact that these English language writers had only limited audiences, but I would have liked to know more about the reach and impact of this work within Uganda.

Chapter Seven sees Kasule switch his focus to popular commercial theatre. He briefly discusses (159) how serious politicized theatre lost much of its audience after the liberalization of early Museveni years, but it seems a shame that no more contemporary straight plays are discussed from here on. Instead we are given a case study of what has been possibly Uganda's most famous popular theatre organization, *The Ebonies*, which has been running since 1977. Similarly to popular performance traditions in other East African nations *The Ebonies* developed as a variety company, engaging with dance, drama and music in often four-to-five hour shows. Here the theatre is produced in multiple languages, is meant primarily for entertainment, but does also engage with a range of social issues. The chapter progresses to study the uniquely Ugandan musical performance form of *Kadongo Kamu* (one guitar, one performer). This 'peoples' musical theatre emerged from the streets to become enormously popular with often dramatized songs performed nearly always by men, frequently satirizing the powerful and expressing the point of view of the poor, though Kasule does recognize that it is often negative in its portrayal of women.

Finally, in Chapter Eight, there is a discussion of Uganda's emerging film industry, *KinaUganda*, based on transcripts of interviews with 'two home movie directors, Miriam Ndagire working in English and Ashraf Simwogerere working in Luganda' (183-4). This is an infant industry. Ndagire has only been making films since 2007. As elsewhere in Africa the industry lacks money and trained personnel, and the films tend to be melodramatic. Sadly, as in the much bigger Nigerian Nollywood, all too often there is a 'tendency to focus on one main narrative – the making of an evil woman' (203). Just why African film has been emerging as so misogynistic and why this is such a popular theme with audiences surely requires investigation and challenge. Kasule shows that, as across the continent, this home movie industry is engaging the talent of many stage actors and drastically, negatively, impacting on the world of live theatre.

All this is well worth reading despite some editing errors, notably on pages 146 and 147 where whole chunks of text are duplicated, the fact that the bibliography is not complete, and that, mystifyingly, on page 144 Kasule entirely incorrectly defines an albatross. However, Chapters One and Two which seek to establish a framework for the text are hugely problematic. Kasule makes a series of generalized assertions which he simply cannot evidence, or indeed which he undermines in the more balanced narrative of the main text. He chooses to read nearly all Ugandan performance as 'inherently political' and 'extremely transgressive' (20), and goes on to variously describe this theatrical transgression as being to 'articulate the concerns of the community'(25), in 'intersections where different texts and styles crisscross' (26), and in 'women's transgression of normative behaviour' (28). While many of the plays at the heart of this book are indeed bravely challenging of political and social injustice, this is by no means universally the case. In relation to women in particular only a minority of the work challenges deeply entrenched Ugandan patriarchy. Moreover the definitions of what constitutes 'transgression' are simply incorrect. Articulating the voice of the people is not in itself transgressive. It may be politically dangerous but that is a different matter. Kasule does his work no favours by trying to read a whole performance tradition through a single lens. His other key concept is that of *katemba*. I had great difficulty in understanding how Kasule was defining this idea as he never pins it down with precise examples. He describes it variously as 'a multi-generic dialogic and hybridized performance form' (28) – what ever that might mean; as 'much concerned with farce' (30) – which at least seems a little more precise, and as 'an interesting convergence, bringing together transgression, spectacle and verbal discourse, memory, politics and performance, and overlapping them with related forms elsewhere in Africa and its diaspora' (30) – which is so all-encompassing as to surely fail as a possible or usable definition. The whole opening section is littered with quotes by cultural theorists from across Africa and indeed other continents entirely which are blithely applied to Ugandan contexts without any evidence of connection being produced. Trying to impose a totalizing radical view on all Ugandan performance does the history of Ugandan theatre and Kasule's own work no favours. I would recommend that the reader simply ignore the opening chapters and move straight to the interesting factual body of the work.

Jane Plastow
University of Leeds

Astrid van Weyenberg, *The Politics of Adaptation: Contemporary African Drama and Greek Tragedy*
Cross/Cultures 165, Amsterdam/New York: Rodopi, 2013
ISBN 978-90-420-3700-7, €56, US$78

Ever since the turn of the millenium, and possibly even earlier, adaptation studies have been on the rise in the humanities. The year 2008 saw the launch of two new journals in the field, *Adaptation* (OUP) and *Journal of Adaptation in Film and Performance* (Intellect), the establishment of the Association of Adaptation Studies, and numerous book publications. Many of these organs do not deal with cultural production from Africa – rather predictably so, their focus largely being on the Anglophone North – even if the continent is not lagging behind in productivity. African adaptations from page to stage can possibly be traced back to mid-seventeenth century *autos* or biblical sketches in today's Portuguese-speaking parts of Africa, although the bulk of material most likely emerged from the mid-twentieth century onwards. Many examples spring to my mind, inner-African adaptations and those related to non-African texts; from Kola Ogunmola's 1963 stage adaptation of Tutuola's *The Palm-wine Drinkard* to Duro Ladipo's 1960s *Eda*, a Yoruba *Everyman*; from 1980s Eritrean dramatizations of Chekhov short stories to Amadina Lihamba's *Hawala ya Fedha* (1980), a Kiswahili play adapted from a novel by Sembene Ousmane (Mwangi 2009). When it comes to adaptations within theatre itself, two categories are the most prominent: adaptations of some of the world's most influential playwrights, such as Shakespeare and Brecht; and adaptations from so-called 'classical genre', particularly Greek tragedy. It is the latter that Astrid van Weyenberg (University of Amsterdam) has chosen for her book-length study on the politics of adaptation in which she analyses six dramatic texts written between 1973 and 2004 by Nigerian and South African playwrights. In four chapters, framed by a substantial introduction and a short, but poignant, conclusion, van Weyenberg discusses plays by Yael Farber, Mark Fleishman, Athol Fugard/John Kani/Winston Ntshona, Wole Soyinka and Femi Osofisan from a dual point of view: how do these plays relate to their Greek source or, rather, what is the dynamic between the these two types of texts; and how do they address the socio-political challenges of the respective moment they deal with. Here, van Weyenberg distinguishes between resistance and revolutionary contexts (Chapters 1-2), and situations of 'post-conflict' and transition (Chapters 3-4). Fugard et al.'s *The Island* (1973)[1] and Osofisan's *Tegonni* (1994) are thus discussed as part of *Antigone*'s refiguration as representative of several political struggles (Chapter 1: African Antigones); Soyinka's *The Bacchae of Euripides* (1972) is read in the context of the playwright's understanding of ritualistic aesthetics and Yoruba tragedy (Chapter 2: Ritual and Revolution); Fleishman's unpublished 'In the City of Paradise' (1998) and Farber's *Morola* (2003), adapted from Aeschylus' *Oresteia* trilogy for a post-apartheid South Africa, are studied in relation to how they dramatize issues arising from the TRC (Chapter 3: Staging Transition); and finally Osofisan's *Women of Owu* (2004) is used as a launching pad for a broader investigation into the theme of mourning. Here, van Weyenberg considers Osofisan not only with reference to Euripides' *Trojan Women* but also in connection to the dramatic texts discussed

---

[1] Dates refer to first productions rather than publication.

earlier on. Greek tragedy, she argues, is still relevant today because contemporary adaptations open up a space for politics and enable a debate that goes beyond an assumed hierarchical constellation between the 'source' and its 'derivatives'. This, we learn, is in itself political because it questions the meaning of 'origin', 'tradition' and 'authority' and helps us understand contemporary African drama and Greek tragedy as equal partners in the debate. Greek tragedy and contemporary African plays are thus connected dialogically rather than in the one-directional flow often favoured by historicist readings.

Hierarchies and binaries are what the author has set out to demolish, and this is not entirely new for adaptation studies on the whole. In fact, adaptation studies have largely come into disciplinary being to debunk the long-held assumption that adaptations are derivative and somewhat 'parasitic' of their source, that they are of less artistic merit by definition, and that 'fidelity' to the perceived original constitutes their principal value. This echoes a similar argument in early postcolonial thought which van Weyenberg gives centre stage in her introduction. Her biggest antagonist is the colonial binary that sees 'African' creative expressions in 'second' position to 'European' cultural texts and that claims ownership of ancient Greece – the presumed pinnacle of artistic merit – to emphasize the apparent superiority of 'Western civilization' (xv). This idealized Eurocentric narrative, much of it rooted in eighteenth- and nineteenth-century thought, van Weyenberg sets out to dismantle, and she does so with great vigour beyond the fifty-page introduction to her book. We are, amongst others, taken through European philosophy, classicist thinking and classical reception studies in her reading of the plays, but also through Afrocentric appropriations which have underscored the influence of African and Asian cultures on ancient Greece. Commendably, she takes cognizance of older, somewhat neglected sources in the debate – James Booth on Wole Soyinka, for example – even if some significant publications in other areas are strangely missing (Catherine Cole's post-2007 publications on the TRC, particularly her monograph *Performing South Africa's Truth Commission* (2010)).

Her qualifications are learned and the whole book is impeccably researched, but the referencing is occasionally relentless. Given that this book emerged out of her PhD thesis this is to be expected, the author being required to demonstrate the width and breadth of her reading. For the reader, however, it can be somewhat tiresome; and there were moments when in the plethora of critical pros and cons I was beginning to lose van Weyenberg as an authorial voice. Now and then I also found her argument slightly reductionist in a reverse sort of way, when she speaks of the plurality of 'African literatures' (xlix) in relation to the apparent singularity of European culture. Nonetheless, the author makes some pertinent points relevant for the study of African adaptations: not all of them are counter-discursive, and not all of them 'write back' to colonialism or a hegemonic West. This is important to keep in mind particularly since I doubt that the playwrights under discussion – many of whom are star dramatists in their own right with international production records – see themselves as writing from and against a position of alleged 'inferiority'. Instead, as van Weyenberg rightly points out, they see Shakespeare and Greek tragedy as part of their own theatrical legacy to be reworked for their own aims and purposes (xlvii; 179), largely with a political, rather than metaphysical or existential, slant (li), with the exception perhaps of Soyinka.

There are some refreshing approaches in this book particularly with regard to general theories of adaptation. For the most part, van Weyenberg resorts to Dutch rather than the standard Anglo-Saxon adaptation theories which provide her (and the reader) with useful new terminology. Following cultural theorist Mieke Bal, she takes to calling the source text 'pre-text' which 'describes a text that precedes, but does not authorize or define [its] re-readings' (xxv). Read through the lens of contemporary adaptations, the pre-text thus becomes 'a changing object' (xxii), rather than a stable point of origin and/or authority. (It also deliciously rings of 'pretence' and 'pretentiousness', if I may be allowed this remark, thus undermining the presumed authority of the source text further.) The idea is to think laterally rather than vertically, and in such a way that our thinking moves dynamically between pre-text and object text rather than take a one-way direction from the 'origin' to the contemporary adaptation. In the same vein, van Weyenberg argues for the contemporary 'object text' (xxv) as the analytical starting point, rather than the source, because it will help us re-evaluate how the past is perceived. Van Weyenberg does not always follow her own advice – 'African Antigones', for example, starts with an analysis of Antigone's western legacy, particularly George Steiner's Antigone study of 1984 – and a lot of her argument seems still geared towards (and against) western receptions of Greek tragedy. Yet I agree with her proposed position. We need to work from the adaptations themselves, and very confidently so, to come to a better understanding of these plays, and the contexts and issues they reflect and address. Only when we abandon this fixation with 'the West' can we begin to analyse African adaptations and their relation to the past, be it linked to politics, metaphysics, theatre or literary genre.

In her readings van Weyenberg focuses only on dramatic texts, not on actual productions or productions contexts, and she does so conscientiously. The most interesting moments in her analysis, however, emerge for me when she considers the 'performative' aspects of a play, such as the meta-theatrical elements in Fugard et al's *The Island*. In future studies this could be elaborated further. I would also like to see an extension of her 'idea of the performative' (xiii) which in the introduction is relegated to a mere footnote (again to Bal), although better explained in her use of Butler in the Antigone chapter. While the Soyinka section on ritualistic aesthetics and Yoruba tragedy will bring little new to those familiar with his works, I really enjoyed how in 'Staging Transition' van Weyenberg reads Fleishman and Farber against each other, rather than successively. It again confirms that these plays are in constant dialogue, and not only with their pre-text.

All in all, van Weyenberg's study is a very timely book that will be useful for both adaptation scholars and those of us working on African theatre. It is to be hoped that it will also advance the study of African adaptations from whichever source, beyond the well-covered contexts of Nigeria and South Africa.

WORK CITED

Mwangi, Evan (2009) 'Amandina Lihamba's Gendered Adaptation of Sembene Ousmane's *The Money-Order*', *Research in African Literatures* 40.3, 149-73.

Christine Matzke
University of Bayreuth

Book Reviews 119

Galina Balashova, *Drama in Modern Ethiopian Literature and Theatre*
Moscow & St Petersburg: Russian Academy of Sciences, Institute of African Studies, 2012
ISBN 9785912980428, Hb $30

Galina Balashova lived in Ethiopia in two stints over a five year period from the late 1960s to 1980, and then conducted research specifically for this project during two official Russian research expeditions in 1991–1992 and again in 2006. She has the notable advantage that she can evidently read and speak Amharic. It is a shame then that this is not a rather better book.

This is not to say that there are not interesting and original findings, or that it will not be of use to subsequent researchers. In Chapter 1 Balashova begins with some fairly cursory descriptions of possible precursors to, and subsequent influences on, Ethiopian drama. Given that all the plays she will discuss in the body of the text were written in Amharic or – a few – in English, the material on the Ethiopian minstrel group, the *azmaris*, and particularly on influential church forms of poetry and music is significant. The very slight material on the performance cultures of other Ethiopian ethnic groups is never considered further and offers few useful insights. She then moves on, as everyone working on this area inevitably does, to the first Ethiopian play, Takle Hawariat's (or in this version Hawaryat's – transcriptions from Amharic tend to vary considerably) *Fabula: Yawreoch Commedia* (Fable: A Comedy of Animals); here just called 'A Comedy'. Although more detailed research on this play has recently emerged (see Abune and Plastow (2010) in *African Theatre: Histories 1850-1950*, and Birhanu and Solomon, forthcoming (2014), *Journal of African Cultural Studies*), Balashova gives useful new detail on staging and commentary by the author. She goes on to discuss in more detail than is available anywhere else the plays of the first court playwrights of the 1930s, Yoftahe Neguse and Melaku Beggo-saw. I found this section of the book particularly interesting as it offers more detailed readings of their key plays than are available anywhere else.

Chapters 2 and 3 deal with the growth of theatre for the elite in the capital, and Chapter 5 with the work of four major playwrights of the late Haile Selassie years of the 1960s and early 1970s: Menghistu Lemma, Tesfaye Gessese, Abe Gubegna (an odd choice as his work was nowhere near the standard of the others in this group) and Ethiopia's pre-eminent playwright, Tseggaye Gebre Medhyn. There is no doubt that this was the golden age of Ethiopian theatre, but it does seem somewhat disproportionate to allot two thirds of the book's analysis to work produced prior to the revolution of 1974. Moreover, while Balashova interviewed some of these playwrights and read the classic early studies of Ethiopian literature which include references to drama; (Gerard 1971, Kane 1975, Molvaer 1980), she has entirely overlooked both the numerous web sources of information on aspects of Ethiopian drama, and my own book, *African Theatre and Politics: the Evolution of Theatre in Ethiopia, Tanzania and Zimbabwe*, Rodopi, 1994, which completely undercuts her claim to have written the first history of Ethiopian theatre.

The final three short chapters look in a most superficial manner at more recent drama, focusing disproportionately on any initiative supported by Russia. So we are told that Getachew Abdi was 'an outstanding playwright, a graduate of [*sic*] State

Institute of Theatrical Arts in Moscow' (132). There is then a single paragraph on his work which by no means evidences how he was 'outstanding'. The playwright given most space in these final chapters; 'the most renowned playwright that generation' (127) [the generation immediately following the revolution] is Ayalneh Mulat, who studied journalism at Moscow State University, and is director of Candlelight Theatre which is funded by the Russian Centre for Culture and Science. Ayalneh Mulat wrote a raft of agit-prop plays and musicals in support of the revolution and has continued to be a most active presence in Ethiopian theatre, but no evidence is given for why he might be considered the 'most renowned' playwright of his generation.

This book is profoundly flawed by its pro-Russian bias and its weak analysis of the politics which have at every stage impacted heavily on Ethiopian theatre, which are discussed with minimal referencing in order to fit in with a Russia-centric view of the world. For example, discussion of British support for the liberation of Ethiopia from Italian occupation in 1940-41 is explained as follows. 'The guerrilla movement in Ethiopia started to receive aid from outside, primarily from the British government, which was planning to strengthen its supremacy in the Indian Ocean with the help of the Ethiopians, and later turn the country into a British protectorate' (55). I am no apologist for British imperialism but in all my research on Ethiopia I have never heard this latter claim and Balashova, as usual in relation to her political analysis, offers no reference to back it up. She also entirely omits the fact that the USSR backed the oppressive regime of the Dergue, which ruled from 1974 to 1991, with massive military support. Indeed the contextualization of the socio-political background to Ethiopian theatre is confused, at times misleading, and refers to almost none other than Russian historians' analysis – and that only seldom. This lack of international research and chauvinistic bias utterly undermines Balashova's credibility as a cultural analyst. She also fails to deal with any theatre other than that produced in the capital of Addis Ababa, and as a result says nothing about the significant amounts of theatre produced in Eritrea while it was an Ethiopian region from 1962 to 1991. Nor does she discuss at all the populist commercial drama of figures such as Iyoel Yohannes who produced over 70 plays at the Hager Fikir Theatre throughout the 1950s and '60s. Presumably these plays are not discussed because they were never published, though this does not account for the entire lack of even a passing mention.

Finally it is a shame that the Russian Institute of African Studies appears to have been unable to find a copy editor who could help render this book into good English. The extremely frequent errors make Balashova's text a trying read. Overall *Drama in Modern Ethiopian Literature and Theatre* gives specialist readers some useful nuggets of information on particular plays and playwrights, but it is a biased, socio-politically misleading and poorly researched book which the reader new to Ethiopian theatre should approach with extreme caution.

Jane Plastow
University of Leeds

Book Reviews 121

Bernth Lindfors, *Ira Aldridge*: Vol. 3, *Performing Shakespeare in Europe, 1852-1855*
Rochester NY: University of Rochester Press, 2013, pp. 350
ISBN 9781580464727, £35

For anyone who knows the excellent first two volumes of this three-volume series on the life of the nineteenth-century American actor Ira Aldridge, it will come as welcome news to learn that Bernth Lindfors has not only completed the set but has also done so in style. For those who don't know the series yet, I can warmly recommend it.

Volume 1 saw young Ira leave the United States for his theatrical apprenticeship in Britain where he plied his trade under an African flag, and we left him in Volume 2 a veteran touring thespian, although still more or less shunned by the London elite and on the brink of turning to Continental Europe to advance his career. Volume 3 takes us with Aldridge on that speculative journey, as the 'African Roscius' assembles a willing but not altogether expert troupe to support him on an expedition that would begin in Brussels and lead them by way of Basel, Berlin, and Vienna to the towns and cities of Prussia and Hungary. It turned out for Aldridge to be what Lindfors describes as 'the most rewarding phase of his career' (6).

While Lindfors sustains the superlative scholarship demonstrated in the earlier books, he changes tack here and narrows his focus. Whereas Volume 1 covers sixteen years and Volume 2 a further nineteen, Volume 3 concentrates on just three. The audiences Aldridge encountered on this tour did not want to see him in the melodramas and farces that dominated his British repertoire but rather in Shakespeare, which he performed in English. As a result, he was known in Continental Europe primarily, though not exclusively, as a Shakespearean actor. Drawing on an impressive range of sources, including many of Aldridge's own letters, Lindfors follows the troupe, and later Aldridge alone, from place to place and investigates, with the help of a trusty band of translators, the reactions he aroused as an 'African' performer of canonical classical roles.

The practicalities and vagaries of the itinerant actors' life are displayed in wonderful close-up, from having to close the debut engagement when an audience of twenty was followed by an audience of none, to escaping the scrutiny of the Austro-Hungarian secret police and making a fortune while being showered with medals and honours by heads of state. There are welcome digressions first into Aldridge's chaotic and lively personal life (he seduced and made pregnant a married woman, for example) and subsequently into comparisons with other contemporary and deceased actors, such as Garrick, Kean, Talma, and Schroder. Even where opinion differed on particulars concerning Aldridge, the 'general feeling,' writes Lindfors, was that he definitely belonged in such a 'distinguished theatrical fraternity' (133).

Towards the end of the book, Lindfors examines in detail how Aldridge played the four parts that came to define his acting in Continental Europe: Othello (perhaps not surprisingly, his most important role and one that divided critics into conservative and liberal wings), Shylock, Macbeth and Richard III, of this group the role he performed the least, as was the case in Britain. Lindfors undertakes important historical reconstruction, and contributes enormously to the debates about Aldridge's 'naturalistic' acting, by looking, as best he can, at what Aldridge did on stage. Noting that the versions of the texts Aldridge performed often lengthened after he had dismissed his British troupe and performed with local companies in multi-lingual productions, Lindfors analyses Aldridge's interpretations through examination of how the actor moved and spoke, the nature of his gestures, and the style of his make-up and costume. Aldridge liked to display his versatility by performing contrasting roles – Macbeth and Othello, for instance – and the main exception to the predominance of Shakespearean characters in these years is the reprisal of his favourite farcical role, Mungo, the black servant in Isaac Bickerstaff's *The Padlock* who speaks in dialect and is dutiful when sober but defiant when drunk. Lindfors argues persuasively that Aldridge took care to appear in this role only after he had performed a serious role 'so that audiences would know he was playing the fool, not seeking to perpetuate a derogatory racial stereotype' (3-4).

Inevitably, Aldridge's life could not, and cannot, be separated from the racism of his time and from the international slave trade and the struggles to end it that framed his life. Lindfors places Aldridge in this context with care, eager to avoid lionizing the pioneer black actor while capturing his complexity as well as the enormity of his achievement. Any debate on his historical standing will find Lindfors' marvellously meticulous portrait of this imposing actor at its heart. There is, however, a decade or so still to go, which, in the volume under review, is wrapped up rather quickly in four pages. Aldridge spent much of the 1860s appearing in Russia and was never to return to the United States as he had planned; he died on tour in Poland in 1867 where he received a state funeral. Lindfors leaves the challenge of the final years to future biographers. Let's hope the wait is not too long. Whoever they may be, they have a hard act to follow.

Colin Chambers
Kingston University

Nadja Keller, Christoph Nix, Thomas Spieckermann (eds) *Theater in Afrika: Zwischen Kunst und Entwicklungszusammenarbeit: Geschichten einer deutsch-malawischen Kooperation / Theatre in Africa: Between Art and Development Cooperation: Stories of a German-Malawian Collaboration (Recherchen 106)*
Berlin: Theater der Zeit, 2013
ISBN 978-3-943881-52-3, $48

In early 2010, a few months before his untimely death, German theatre maker Christoph Schlingensief laid the foundation stone of what was arguably his most ambitious project: the building of an opera village near Ouagadougou in Burkina Faso. Long before his vision of an artistic centre combining an opera house with schools and hospitals started to take shape in the West African savannah, one of Germany's most controversial artists had managed to spark a hype, encouraging German mass media to regularly report on an African country beyond their usual focus on crisis and war.

It was now that the Stadttheater – the German system of state- and municipality-subsidized theatres – 'discovered' the African continent and suddenly recognized the potential inherent in collaborating with African partners. Organizations like the German Federal Cultural Foundation, one of Germany's most important funders of art and culture, started increasingly to support projects including the participation of African artists or arts institutions.

On the one hand, this sudden interest of theatre makers in anything 'African' raises legitimate questions about the artistic sincerity of some of them. As the manager of a municipal theatre recently confessed to me when asking advice about possible cooperation partners: 'I don't know anything about Africa and, to be honest, I don't care – but I want the funding!' On the other hand, the orientation of arts funders and subsidized theatres towards Africa provides some artists with longstanding ties to the continent with the opportunity to finally put their commitment, at least temporarily, on a sound financial base.

One such example is Christoph Nix, theatre manager at Theater Konstanz. Working in African countries for many years without external support, the Federal Cultural Foundation finally provided Nix and his theatre with funding for a three-year collaboration with the Nanzikambe Arts theatre group in Blantyre, Malawi. While the first year of the cooperation consisted of workshops in Germany and Malawi, the second year saw the exchange of plays from both countries. The third year, finally, culminated in the joint development of a play, assembling a mixed ensemble of actors as well as a director from Germany and Malawi, respectively.

The bilingual (German/English), edited volume *Theatre in Africa: Between Art and Development Cooperation: Stories of a German-Malawian Collaboration* – follows *Theatre in Sub-Saharan Africa* (Hemke, 2010) as the second volume the renowned publishing house Theater der Zeit has dedicated to African theatre within four years – and describes this collaboration from various perspectives.

In fourteen essays, authors from both countries – among them actors, directors, journalists, economists, political scientists and even the German Minister of Foreign Affairs – present their view on *Crossing Borders, from Lake to Lake*, as the joint project was called in reference to Lake Malawi and Lake Constance. The bilingual structure of the volume offers eight originally German- and six English-language texts with their respective translations. Since these translations unfortunately represent rather brief summaries of the original, only bilingual readers will get the full benefit of the book.

The book is in two parts: while the first one describes the project from an artistic and organizational perspective, the second one classifies the endeavour within the bigger framework of development cooperation. According to the editors (besides Nix himself Thomas Spieckermann and Nadja Keller, two collaborators from Theater Konstanz), the publication aims at providing impulses for other cultural institutions that consider international cooperation.

In the first part, Thomas Spieckermann, co-editor and head of dramaturgy at Theater Konstanz, gives an impressive account on how the mixed group's joint experience of political unrest in Malawi changes the character of the project. While in the beginning, the collaboration focuses on the personal experience of the participating artists and their different aesthetic approaches, larger questions about how theatre can play a relevant part in a rapidly changing society take centre stage as the project evolves. Another editor of the book, and project manager for African partnerships at Theater Konstanz, Nadja Keller, contrasts the German subsidized theatre system with the reality theatre makers face in Malawi. At the same time, she vividly describes the administrative challenges an international collaboration is confronted with.

Also in the first part, director Thokozani Kapiri describes the balancing act of Malawian theatre makers trying to negotiate their own aesthetic conceptions with the oftentimes patronizing policy of foreign donor organizations. His German counterpart and co-director of the joint production, Clemens Bechtel, gives insights into the tensions within the international ensemble, discussing the difficult realization of equality in a co-production of economically unequal partners. While most contributors confine their critique to the broader contexts surrounding the project – like arts funding, the situation of theatre in Malawi or development cooperation in general – Bechtel is one of two authors who critically discuss the project itself and their own role in it. The other positive exception in this regard is actor Yannick Zürcher. From a very personal perspective, Zürcher describes the process of the project as the deconstruction of dearly held clichés and concepts of identity. The otherwise predominant praise of the project, however, at times gives the publication the sound of an anniversary speech. While the immediacy and directness of inside perspectives from people involved in the project definitely accounts for one of the strengths of the book, a more self-critical approach would have provided the publication with more depth.

The second part, finally, positions the project within the larger framework of development cooperation. Economist Rolf Kappel, Zurich-based professor for the problems of developing countries, comprehensively summarizes the common scientific explanations for the prosperity gap between the global North and South, highlighting the importance of institutional change in many countries of the so-called developing world. Bernd Eisenblätter, former spokesman of the GIZ (German Society for International Cooperation), emphasizes the significance of intercultural competence for international cooperation. Both authors convincingly discuss the role the arts and theatre can play in this regard.

Malawian theatre scholar Smith Likongwe's contribution and Kirstin Mbohwa-Pagels' interview of Zilanie Gondwe-Nyundo – the former led the Goethe-Institute in Malawi during the three years of its existence, the latter is the chair of the Malawian branch of the pan-African arts association Arterial Network – provide good introductions into the cultural policy background of Africa in general and Malawi in particular.

In conclusion, the volume provides a concise overview of the discourses influencing international cooperation within the arts in Africa. From an academic point of view, the publication remains rather descriptive and lacks profound analysis. With regard to the defined goal of providing impulses for other cultural institutions, a more self-critical reflection would have been useful. Nevertheless, the volume represents a good read for anyone who is looking for a solid introduction into the manifold aspects of international theatre work.

Laurenz Leky
africologneFESTIVAL, Theater im Bauturm, Cologne

Yvette Hutchison, *South African Performance and Archives of Memory*
Manchester and New York: Manchester University Press, 2013
ISBN 978 0 7190 8373 0, np

This volume will certainly be a valuable addition to scholars and students engaged with the particular questions around South Africa and the Truth and Reconciliation Commission and transition in the post-1994 era. Hutchison engages with this terrain with the thoughtful perspectives of a vigilant observer. The book seeks also to provoke considerations around performance, archives and memories; in particular, as she indicates, those performances which participate in 'nation building'. She comments, with the sensibility of an insider, on the 'realistic constructivist nature of national identity' familiar to South Africans (5).

The two elements of the book are at times quite closely interwoven, insofar as the global debates about memory, archives and historical violence inform the introductory chapter. The 'exceptionalism' of the South African case, so much inside the sensibilities and rhetorics of the anti-apartheid movement, comes into contact here with several other, distinct exceptionalisms. The Holocaust, the Vietnam War, the Algerian War, and Latin America are invoked in the Introduction, but Hutchison's study is not a trans-national one: her focus is on the performance traditions of South Africa, and invoking Austin, she situates 'performance' within the sequence of utterances which effect change in the world (17).

These interpretive strategies are not new; and the tradition of commentary on the Truth and Reconciliation Commission has from its early days been identified as conjoining of theatricality and 'performativity' in the staging of passage that both precipitated and documented the testimonial collectivity of South Africans, who were, after all, conjuring into being the New South Africa. Testimony was individual and collective, proving some instrument of the therapeutic, while conjuring up a national subject of a particular kind.

Hutchison's chapters on the Truth and Reconciliation Commission (TRC) in some ways address terrain material discussed in Catherine Cole's important study, *Performing South Africa's Truth Commission* (Bloomington: Indiana University Press, 2010); though there is significant difference in the orientation of the two books. Cole's work engages with the TRC at the point of intersection of performance studies and legal theory; whereas Hutchison is considering the cycle of testimonial events in order to consider the staging of memory as a private domain of holding as well as its performance as national archive. It seems to me that both authors make a valuable contribution to the debate and to the generation of critically engaged thinking about transitional justice, particularly as it seems that there is in this moment a proliferation of suggested Commissions in both northern and southern hemispheres. The South African instance is often invoked as a template, and it seems to me the more nuanced our understanding of the specificity of the TRC and its strategies and purposes, the better.

Hutchison does hold up a rich assortment of theatrical experiment for scrutiny, and it is significant to see the spectrum of artistic engagement in the performance arena. The Magnet Theatre Company, Mike van Graan, Handspring Puppet Company, Brett Bailey's 'Third World Bun Fight' and Yael Farber are all made available to an international critical audience: this in itself is a significant contribution both to regional studies and to post-colonial analysis. Her orientation toward the questions around national formation, draws theorists of empire into dialogue with theatre scholars as well as urban planners, archivists, anthropologists, and museologists. The city, the museum, and the gallery are, along with the theatre all sites through which the transitional process is being performed. Further touchstones that provoked particular performance idioms are also invoked. Hutchison discusses Thabo Mbeki's 'African Renaissance' and the Timbuktu archive as a particular point in the South African pan-African resurgence at the turn of the millennium; as well as the staging of the distinctively global (and post-African) vision of the 'Rainbow Nation' staged during the period of the World Cup in 2010. Those contradictory representations point to the inchoate and transitional character of the New South Africa, which, having come out of its States of Emergency, is still very much in its emergence. Hutchison's diversity of enquiry is a valuable one for cultural critics who are all-too-aware of the pressure within South Africa to 'invent' a country that will be responsible to its pasts while constructing its future.

It is therefore something of a shame that there are several editorial oversights that should have been addressed. The historian Philippe Ariès is misspelled as Aries; and there is rather too much dependence on second-hand sources in the Introduction. The Ariès is cited via Hutton; and Frederic Bartlett and Robert Pope are both cited via Oliver Sacks' *An Anthropologist on Mars*; the oversight is frustrating because there is no listing in the bibliography of the primary sources from which Sacks draws, so the trail is difficult to follow. J.L. Austin, who is at the centre of Hutchison's enquiry is mentioned in the text but does not appear either in the bibliography nor is 'speech-act theory' listed in the index. Hutchison's discussion of Benedict Anderson's *Imagined Communities* and its relation to Hobsbawm and Ranger gives the Anderson date as '2006'; clearly this is the edition to which Hutchison is referring; however the work was written in 1983, the same year as Hobsbawm and Ranger's *Invention of Tradition* (which is given that date, in the discussion). The dating anomalies make that intellectual encounter illegible for a young scholar. (The Anderson is cited twice in the bibliography, one dating from 1991; the other the 2006 edition. By the way, the bibliography listing is erroneously given as Hobsba*wn*, E. and Ranger, T.)

One final comment on the narrating of history: Hutchison glosses the South African story in the following terms: 'The history of South Africa has been a history of struggle: against the elements and wild animals, while various ethnic groups both from within and beyond South Africa have fought one another for autonomy and control of the country's rich natural resources' (95).

This summative statement does not account for the massive asymmetries within the historical and political arena, which the TRC and Hutchison's own analyses highlight. The performance of Apartheid South Africa sought to deny communities access to the law on the basis of racial classification. That is the question addressed by Catherine Cole's study cited earlier.

Jane Taylor
University of Leeds

Book Reviews 127

Kene Igweonu and Osita Okagbue (eds) *Performative Inter-Actions in African Theatre*
Newcastle upon Tyne: Cambridge Scholars Publishing, 2013
ISBN 1-4438-5611-8, np

The three volumes in this series offer a range of essays on three topics. *Diaspora Representations and the Interweaving of Cultures – Innovation, Creativity and Social Change – Making Space, Rethinking Drama and Theatre in Africa*. The editors have assembled a range of international scholars offering ten essays in each volume, creating a stimulating forum for the discussion of each theme. *African Theatre* will hope to carry a more detailed review in a subsequent issue.

Martin Banham

Notice on a forthcoming title

Alain Ricard, *Wole Soyinka et Nestor Zinsou: De la scène à l'espace public*
Paris: Karthala, 2014 forthcoming

A comparative study of the works and lives of the two writers, Soyinka from Nigeria, and Zinsou from Togo, against the political and cultural developments in their two countries...and more specifically, a study of Zinsou through Soyinka. Alain Ricard's take-off point is the two authors' similar background: in the fact that they were both strongly influenced by the Yoruba culture – Soyinka more directly by birth, and Zinsou by being brought up in the Yoruba quarters of Lomé. Zinsou's subsequent development was of course very much francophone, and his models were the classical French writers, but he soon felt dissatisfied with these and turned back to his early experiences. Then he became embroiled in politics, was briefly in the legislative assembly, till the military, backed by France, seized power through truncated elections. Following the violent protests that followed, Zinsou had to flee into exile in Germany, where he has been now for some twenty years. In the '80s, his works as a dramatist dominated the scene, but he seems now to have left the stage and writes more fiction.

The similarities with Soyinka's work and life are clear, and Alain Ricard writes about them with his usual lucidity, in simple flowing prose devoid of the usual academic jargons (very reminiscent in fact of Kaye Whiteman on Lagos), bringing in many personal details and cross-references from his intimate knowledge of the writers' works as well as of the socio-political history of Gulf of Benin. Given that Ricard has lived and travelled and taught literature in this region much over the past forty or so years, and has therefore made a considerable number of acquaintances in the process, it is hardly surprising that the book is rich in information and full of refreshing analyses. It is also a bold and welcome venture, in that such comparative studies in the literature of these two countries are very rare indeed and, hopefully, will inspire more like it in the future.

Femi Osofisan

www.ingramcontent.com/pod-product-compliance
Lightning Source LLC
Chambersburg PA
CBHW070808230426
43665CB00017B/2536